CLASSICS IN EDUCATION
Lawrence A. Cremin, General Editor

☆  ☆  ☆

THE REPUBLIC AND THE SCHOOL
Horace Mann on the Education of Free Men
*Edited by Lawrence A. Cremin*

AMERICAN IDEAS ABOUT ADULT EDUCATION
1710–1951
*Edited by C. Hartley Grattan*

DEWEY ON EDUCATION
*Introduction and Notes by Martin S. Dworkin*

THE SUPREME COURT AND EDUCATION
(Revised and Enlarged)
*Edited by David Fellman*

INTERNATIONAL EDUCATION
A Documentary History
*Edited by David G. Scanlon*

CRUSADE AGAINST IGNORANCE
Thomas Jefferson on Education
*Edited by Gordon C. Lee*

CHINESE EDUCATION UNDER COMMUNISM
*Edited by Chang-tu Hu*

CHARLES W. ELIOT AND POPULAR EDUCATION
*Edited by Edward A. Krug*

WILLIAM T. HARRIS ON EDUCATION
(in preparation)
*Edited by Martin S. Dworkin*

THE *EMILE* OF JEAN JACQUES ROUSSEAU
Selections
*Translated and Edited by William Boyd*

THE MINOR EDUCATIONAL WRITINGS OF
JEAN JACQUES ROUSSEAU
*Selected and Translated by William Boyd*

**PSYCHOLOGY AND THE SCIENCE OF EDUCATION**
Selected Writings of Edward L. Thorndike
*Edited by Geraldine M. Joncich*

**THE NEW-ENGLAND PRIMER**
*Introduction by Paul Leicester Ford*

**BENJAMIN FRANKLIN ON EDUCATION**
*Edited by John Hardin Best*

**THE COLLEGES AND THE PUBLIC**
1787–1862
*Edited by Theodore Rawson Crane*

**TRADITIONS OF AFRICAN EDUCATION**
*Edited by David G. Scanlon*

**NOAH WEBSTER'S AMERICAN SPELLING BOOK**
*Introductory Essay by Henry Steele Commager*

**VITTORINO DA FELTRE
AND OTHER HUMANIST EDUCATORS**
By William Harrison Woodward
*Foreword by Eugene F. Rice, Jr.*

**DESIDERIUS ERASMUS
CONCERNING THE AIM AND METHOD
OF EDUCATION**
By William Harrison Woodward
*Foreword by Craig R. Thompson*

**JOHN LOCKE ON EDUCATION**
*Edited by Peter Gay*

**CATHOLIC EDUCATION IN AMERICA**
A Documentary History
*Edited by Neil G. McCluskey, S.J.*

**THE AGE OF THE ACADEMIES**
*Edited by Theodore R. Sizer*

**HEALTH, GROWTH, AND HEREDITY**
G. Stanley Hall on Natural Education
*Edited by Charles E. Strickland and Charles Burgess*

**TEACHER EDUCATION IN AMERICA**
A Documentary History
*Edited by Merle L. Borrowman*

THE EDUCATED WOMAN IN AMERICA
Selected Writings of Catharine Beecher,
Margaret Fuller, and M. Carey Thomas
*Edited by Barbara M. Cross*

EMERSON ON EDUCATION
Selections
*Edited by Howard Mumford Jones*

ECONOMIC INFLUENCES UPON EDUCATIONAL
PROGRESS IN THE UNITED STATES, 1820–1850
By Frank Tracy Carlton
*Foreword by Lawrence A. Cremin*

QUINTILIAN ON EDUCATION
*Selected and Translated by William M. Smail*

ROMAN EDUCATION FROM CICERO
TO QUINTILIAN
By Aubrey Gwynn, S.J.

HERBERT SPENCER ON EDUCATION
*Edited by Andreas M. Kazamias*

JOHN LOCKE'S *OF THE CONDUCT
OF THE UNDERSTANDING*
*Edited by Francis W. Garforth*

STUDIES IN EDUCATION DURING THE
AGE OF THE RENAISSANCE, 1400–1600
By William Harrison Woodward
*Foreword by Lawrence Stone*

JOHN AMOS COMENIUS ON EDUCATION
*Introduction by Jean Piaget*

HUMANISM AND THE SOCIAL ORDER
IN TUDOR ENGLAND
By Fritz Caspari

VIVES' *INTRODUCTION TO WISDOM*
*Edited by Marian Leona Tobriner, S.N.J.M.*

THE THEORY OF EDUCATION IN
THE *REPUBLIC* OF PLATO
By Richard Lewis Nettleship
*Foreword by Robert McClintock*

**UTOPIANISM AND EDUCATION**
Robert Owen and the Owenites
*Edited by John F. C. Harrison*

**SCHOOLS OF HELLAS**
By Kenneth J. Freeman
*Foreword by William M. Calder III*

**THE EDUCATIONAL THEORIES
OF THE SOPHISTS**
*Edited by James L. Jarrett*

**SIR THOMAS ELYOT'S**
*THE BOOK NAMED THE GOVERNOR*
*Abridged and Edited by John M. Major*

**JEWISH EDUCATION IN THE UNITED STATES**
A Documentary History
*Edited by Lloyd P. Gartner*

**HENRY BARNARD'S** *SCHOOL ARCHITECTURE*
*Edited by Jean and Robert McClintock*

**JOHN STUART MILL ON EDUCATION**
*Edited by Francis W. Garforth*

**RICHARD MULCASTER'S** *POSITIONS*
*Abridged and Edited by Richard L. DeMolen*

**PIONEERS OF MODERN EDUCATION
IN THE SEVENTEENTH CENTURY**
By John William Adamson
*Foreword by Joan Simon*

**THE GREAT AWAKENING AND AMERICAN EDUCATION**
A Documentary History
*Edited by Douglas Sloan*

**JOSEPH LANCASTER AND THE
MONITORIAL SCHOOL MOVEMENT**
A Documentary History
*Edited by Carl F. Kaestle*

**AMERICAN EDUCATION AND VOCATIONALISM**
A Documentary History
*Edited by Marvin Lazerson and W. Norton Grubb*

**SIR JAMES KAY-SHUTTLEWORTH
ON POPULAR EDUCATION**
*Edited by Trygve R. Tholfsen*

# Chinese Education under Communism

Edited, with an Introduction and Notes, by
CHANG–TU HU

SECOND EDITION

CLASSICS IN

No. 7

EDUCATION

TEACHERS COLLEGE PRESS
TEACHERS COLLEGE, COLUMBIA UNIVERSITY
NEW YORK AND LONDON

# Preface

There has always been a paradox about revolutions: on the one hand, they represent a break with history; on the other hand, they are inevitably circumscribed by history. No matter how much the revolutionary seeks to "overthrow all existing social conditions," he finds himself, willy-nilly, a creature of time and place, of folkway and tradition. Thus, in our own era, it has been something of a cliché to remark that the Russian revolution becomes more Russian and less of a revolution as the years pass. And thus, too, we note the fascinating counterpoint of change and continuity as the Chinese Communists seek to escape from two thousand years of history.

Professor Hu is ever aware of this paradox as he traces the massive reform of Chinese education during the past ten years. He is dealing with an enterprise of unsurpassed dimensions, involving, according to government statistics, well-nigh 100,000,000 students in a vast variety of schools, and even greater numbers beyond the schools. Moreover, it is an enterprise infused throughout with the missionary zeal of Communist ideology. The goal, as Mr. Lu Ting-Yi, Chief of the Propaganda Department of the Chinese Communist Party's Central Committee once indicated, is nothing less than the total overturn of "old traditions in educational work that have persisted for thousands of years." Whether the effort will succeed remains to be seen; the fact is that impressive strides have been made to date, and, as Professor Hu persuasively contends, we cannot understand the contemporary world apart from them.

Lawrence A. Cremin

# Contents

TRADITION AND CHANGE IN
    CHINESE EDUCATION
      by CHANG-TU HU          1

1. ON PRACTICE
    by Mao Tse-tung       79

2. HOW TO BE A GOOD COMMUNIST
    by Liu Shao-ch'i       90

3. ON THE NEW DEMOCRACY
    by Mao Tse-tung       100

4. ON THE CORRECT HANDLING OF CONTRADICTIONS
    AMONG THE PEOPLE
    by Mao Tse-tung       104

5. IN REFUTATION OF AN ANTISOCIALIST SCIENTIFIC
    PROGRAM
    by Kuo Mo-jo       108

6. ACTIVELY CARRY OUT THE REFORM OF THE
    SCHOOL SYSTEM TO BRING ABOUT GREATER,
    FASTER, BETTER, AND MORE ECONOMICAL RESULTS
    IN THE DEVELOPMENT OF EDUCATION
    by Yang Hsiu-feng       122

7. EDUCATION MUST BE COMBINED WITH PRODUCTIVE
    LABOR
    by Lu Ting-yi       139

8. OUR SCHOOLING SYSTEM MUST BE REFORMED
    by Lu Ting-yi       154

x    *Contents*

9. EDUCATIONAL REVOLUTION AND PROGRESS:
   1949-1959
   *by Yang Hsiu-feng*                                    170

10. DOWN WITH THE FOUNTAINHEAD OF REVISIONIST
    EDUCATION
    *by Shih Yen-hung*                                    182

11. THE WAY TO TRAIN ENGINEERING AND TECHNI-
    CAL PERSONNEL AS VIEWED FROM THE SHANGHAI
    MACHINE TOOL PLANT
    *from* People's Daily                                 198

12. A NEW TYPE OF SCHOOL THAT COMBINES
    THEORY WITH PRACTICE
    *from* Kiangsi Daily                                  211

13. TAKING ALL SOCIETY AS THEIR FACTORY:
    PEKING UNIVERSITY'S ACHIEVEMENTS IN
    EDUCATIONAL REVOLUTION IN THE LIBERAL
    ARTS
    *from* Peking Review                                  224

# Tradition and Change
# in Chinese Education

By CHANG–TU HU

## I

The triumph of Communism on the mainland of China has had world-wide repercussions. It has not only resulted in a fundamental shift in the world balance of power but it has also given rise to many political, military, and economic problems of the first magnitude, the solution of which will, for some time to come, continue to tax the best minds the world over. Important though the international ramifications are, the true significance of the Chinese Communist revolution lies first of all in what the Communists have done and plan to do to transform the most populous nation on earth.

During the past decade or so, a considerable body of literature has accumulated on the political structure, economic development, military potential, and foreign policy of China under Communism. Yet, the vital problem of education, through which the transformation of the Chinese nation must in the long run be realized, has been only scantily and haphazardly treated. It is in recognition of this deficiency that the documents that follow were selected in order to show, in the words of the Communist leaders, the fundamental considerations and principles of education in the regime under their control, as well as the concrete educational policies based thereon.

There can be little doubt that, aside from purely domestic consequences of the new educational principles and practices in China, there are world implications

1

which we ignore at our own risk. First the Russian Sputnik, and later the Gagarin and Titov feats, aroused in many Westerners a desire to learn more about the Soviet educational system which has been represented by the Soviet regime as an indubitable proof of the superiority of Soviet Socialism. Although it is difficult to determine the effect of this claim to educational superiority on the rest of the world, especially on the underdeveloped countries, few would deny that education has become an important part of the larger struggle between East and West, on the outcome of which so much depends. Bearing this in mind, the Chinese educational experiment in transforming the nation assumes considerable significance, because it is likely to exert greater influence on the younger and less-developed nations with which China, and not the Soviet Union, seems to have a good deal in common.

One dominant fact of contemporary Chinese national life is the radical changes which have been brought about, and it is this that has earned for the Communists the epithet of revolutionaries. This revolutionary characteristic becomes more meaningful when it is recalled that the Chinese have long been regarded as the most rebellious but the least revolutionary of peoples. In both scope and intensity, the Chinese Communist revolution has few parallels in world history; indeed, for ten years after the new regime's accession to power, almost all the familiar adjectives used to describe things Chinese have lost their meaning. It is no longer the "sick man of the East"; it is no longer "a country of peasants"; it is no longer "a land ruled by scholars"; indeed, it appears to be not even "peace-loving." The violently emotional American reaction to a friendly China turned enemy is, in no small measure, attributable to the abruptness and finality with which revolutionary China has changed its international postures.

Traditional China had many features peculiar to that ancient civilization, but students of Sinology have always been impressed with one outstanding feature that has variously been called continuity, stability, changelessness, or historical stagnation. Disregarding the choice of words, it can hardly be disputed that traditional China was, for more than two thousand years, charcterized by the absence of changes of fundamental nature. Inasmuch as education plays a decisive role in the formation and transformation of any nation, the phenomenon of China's past traditionalism and present-day revolution can be better understood through an examination of the development in Chinese education.

## EDUCATION IN TRADITIONAL CHINA

"Because a nation seeks through education to mold the character of its citizens and so reflects its aims—political, social, economic, and cultural—a study of its educational system can contribute as richly to an understanding of its aims in general as a direct study of its political policies." So wrote I. L. Kandel.[1] In traditional China, perhaps more than in any other old civilization, education was considered the primary, if not the sole, means by which the character of its citizens was molded. Chinese emphasis on education has been proverbial, for a readily understandable reason. It formed the very foundation on which rested the entire political, social, economic, and cultural life of the Chinese people.

Two complementary cultural factors were responsible for the tremendous stress on education. In the negative sense, the Chinese had at a relatively early stage freed themselves from rigorous religious considerations, hence "no religious creed, no ecclesiastical authority was allowed for more than a brief period to dominate the political state."[2] The absence of an essentially religious orientation to life rendered secular education, as a form of human effort toward the achievement of the aims of life, that much more imperative. The other side of the

[1] I. L. Kandel, *The New Era in Education* (Boston: Houghton Mifflin Company, 1955), p. 13.

[2] Sir George Sansom, *The Western World and Japan* (New York: Alfred A. Knopf, 1951), p. 463. Here Sir George discusses education in Japan, but what he says about Japan is essentially true of China.

same cultural coin is traditional Chinese humanism which placed the orderly conduct of human affairs in *this* world and the regulating of human relations above everything else. This required the nurturing, training, conditioning, and, in modern parlance, the ideological molding of the Chinese people to accept and perpetuate a set of humanistic values which must find expression in all aspects of Chinese life. Therefore, traditional Chinese education, both in theory and in practice, was carried on within the framework of a dominant ideology, commonly referred to as Confucianism.

## THE CONFUCIAN CONCEPT OF EDUCATION

In discussing Confucianism in the context of Chinese traditional education, two points need clarification at the outset. One is that Confucianism, as a system of thought, represented only one of many schools which at the time of Confucius (551–479 B.C.) and after contended with one another for universal acceptance and dominance. Even after its ascendancy to the position of dominance in the Earlier Han period (202 B.C. to 9 A.D.), other schools—Taoism, which is primarily known for its mysticism and advocacy of inaction; Legalism, which stressed the legalistic approach to government and social control; and later Buddhism—continued to exert influence on Chinese thinking at various times to a greater or less degree. The second point is that Confucianism, contrary to popular belief, is not a religion, although it contains certain elements which lend themselves to religious interpretation. Fung Yu-lan, a well-known Chinese philosopher, wrote that "Confucianism is no more a religion than, say, Platonism or Aristotelianism. It is true that the Four Books have been the Bible of the Chinese people, but in the Four Books there is no story of creation, and no mention of a heaven or hell."[3]

The ultimate goal of Confucian education is the per-

---

[3] Fung Yu-lan, *A Short History of Chinese Philosophy*, translated by Derk Bodde (New York: The Macmillan Company, 1948), p. 1.

fection of man in the ethical sense. *The Great Learning*, one of the Four Books which constitute the Confucian scripture, begins with the following:

What the Great Learning teaches, is—to illustrate illustrious virtue; to renovate the people; and to rest in the highest excellence. . . . The Ancients, who wished to illustrate illustrious virtue throughout the kingdom, first ordered well their own states. Wishing to order well their states, they first regulated their families. Wishing to regulate their families, they first cultivated their persons. Wishing to cultivate their persons, they first rectified their hearts. Wishing to rectify their hearts, they first sought to be sincere in their thoughts. Wishing to be sincere in their thoughts, they first extended to the utmost their knowledge. Such extension of knowledge lay in the investigation of things.[4]

There is thus an escalating scheme leading to the illustration of perfect virtue throughout the kingdom, which really means the world or humanity at large.[5] The attainment of this and other goals, however, must begin with the investigation of things and the extension of knowledge, both of which are clearly educational endeavors. There is, therefore, a firm belief in the universality of education, because all the larger organized units of human beings, whether the family or the state, are composed of individuals on whose moral rectitude the well-being of the larger units depends. It was this belief in the universality of education that prompted Confucius to declare that "in education, there are no class distinctions."[6] Also, it was this belief that distinguished traditional Chinese education from education in the West where even today the age-old conflict between the humanist and rationalist philosophies on the one hand and the Christian school of thought on the other, still manifests its influence in many countries—"that one centered the curriculum of the elementary schools designed for the

4 *The Great Learning.*

5 The Chinese words which Legge translated as "kingdom" are *T'ien-hsia*, literally "heaven below," or "under heaven," meaning the whole of mankind.

6 Liu Wu-chi, *Confucius, His Life and Time* (New York: Philosophical Library, 1955), chap. 8.

poor around Christianity and that of the schools for the privileged around the classics."[7]

Profoundly humanistic, the Confucian philosophy of education had as its object the achievement of universal tranquillity through the cultivation of what Confucius termed *Jen,* or the quality of humanness. In *The Analects,* another of the Four Books, the word *Jen* appears over a hundred times, forming the thesis of no less than fifty-eight chapters. "The determined scholar and the man of virtue will not seek to live at the expense of injuring their humanness. They will even sacrifice their lives to preserve their humanness complete."[8] Such is the quality expected of a scholar, or of an educated man. In the Confucian way of thinking, therefore, education is a process through which man realizes his intrinsic value and dignity as an individual human being and seeks to arrive at a state of harmony with both humanity and nature. Consequently, when a man possesses the quality of humanness, there can be no doubt about his being a loyal subject to his ruler, a filial son to his parents, and a faithful friend to his friends. The state of *Jen* or humanness, being the ultimate of virtue, was equated by Confucius with sagehood which he considered himself incapable of attaining, as he declared: "The sage and the man of perfect virtue: how dare I rank myself with them? It may simply be said of me, that I strive to become such without satiety, and teach others without weariness."[9]

The moral goal of *Jen* in Confucian context may thus be compared with the state of sainthood in the Christian tradition; neither can be properly regarded as aims of education. While Christian ethics leading to salvation became the aim for the Christian West, the training of a *chun-tzu* or superior man became the aim for Confucian China. If the concept of *Jen* were too abstract and obscure for man to aspire to, much less to attain, the ideal

7 Robert Ulich, *The Education of Nations* (Cambridge, Mass.: Harvard University Press, 1961), p. 3.

8 *The Analects.*

9 *Ibid.*

of *chun-tzu* is more concrete and within the realm of educational objectives. In the words of Confucius, a *chun-tzu* or superior man possesses these qualities: "The superior man, extensively studying all learning, and keeping himself under the restraint of the rules of propriety, may thus likewise not overstep what is right"; "the superior man has neither anxiety nor fear"; "the superior man in everything considers righteousness to be essential. He performs the act of righteousness according to the rules of propriety. He brings it forth in humility. He completes it with sincerity."[10]

It may be said that the Confucian concept of education was founded on the ethical and philosophical principle of *Jen,* with the cultivation and education of superior man as its primary purpose, aiming ultimately at the orderly regulation of human affairs in accordance with the *Tao* or Way of Nature itself.

## EDUCATION AND TRADITIONAL SOCIETY AND GOVERNMENT

However noble and desirable the Confucian ideal of universal education may have been, the socioeconomic conditions of traditional China, like all other societies at a similar stage of development, permitted only a small minority of the population to receive education in the formal sense. Socially and politically, the status of being educated, which entitled a person to be designated a *chun-tzu,* carried with it both prestige and power. This is particularly significant when it is remembered that traditional China at no time developed a hereditary aristocracy based on birth, wealth, or religious considerations. Throughout the ages, the Confucian ideal of leaving the reins of government and social control in the hands of the morally superior or educated members of the society persisted, thus making traditional Chinese society, at least in theory, an open one, the sole criterion for upward mobility being proved ability through education. To be sure, there were periods of time in Chinese

10 *Ibid.*

history when this ideal was made mockery of, when sheer force was employed for political ascendancy, when governmental power was abused to such an extent that rebellions became inevitable, and when the educated, as members of the ruling group, pursued only personal ends. Such periods of political disunity, social disintegration, and economic dislocation alternated with periods of good and effective government, peace and relative prosperity, forming a pattern which has been aptly described as the Chinese dynastic cycle. In spite of this alternation between peace and upheaval, the underlying Confucian ideal that government must be by moral rectitude and example was never seriously challenged, hence the remarkable continuity in the adherence to the Confucian concept of education.

There was, in a historical context, a close correlation between the conditions of the country at a given period and the degree to which the Confucian code of ethics was adhered to by the people in general and by the educated class in particular. The preservation or downfall of the Chinese dynasty, therefore, was dependent on the acceptance or rejection of the Confucian ideals by the educated elite, not only in name, but in practice as well. Likewise, the well-being of the society as a whole was determined by the moral fiber of the society, for which the educated elite was expected to assume primary responsibility. By setting personal examples, the educated few taught and promoted the virtues of filial piety, loyalty to the ruler, humanheartedness, faithfulness, and other Confucian ethical principles. The true value of education was in the belief that education provided the only avenue to moral superiority which, in turn, was regarded as the sole qualification for participation in government and social leadership.

Implicit in this principle was the assumption that human society was composed of two complementary groups which, in educational terms, were represented by the *chun-tzu* or superior man, on the one hand, and the *hsiao-jen* or mean man, on the other. This dichotomy, in the Confucian context, is subject to two different interpretations, with one justifying the other. Socially and politically, the superior man is a member of the ruling group, or simply a ruler, while a mean man is to be ruled. Hence "the carrying of burdens is a task for the mean men, whereas the carriage is a vehicle for the superior men";[11] and "when a superior man is well instructed, he loves men; when a mean man is well instructed, he is easily ruled."[12] Morally, "the superior man has a dignified ease without pride; the mean man has pride without a dignified ease"; and "the progress of the superior man is upwards; the progress of the mean man is downwards."[13] In short, the superior man is the ruler, by virtue of his moral superiority. This class theory was further enunciated by the second most important Confucian philosopher, Mencius, who stated:

Some labor with their brains and some labor with their brawn. Those who labor with their brains govern others; those who labor with their brawn are governed by others. Those governed by others, feed them. Those who govern others, are fed by them. This is a universal principle in the world. . . . If there were no men of a superior grade, there would be no one to rule the countrymen. If there were no countrymen, there would be no one to support the men of superior grade.[14]

On the shoulders of the educated fell the dual task of direct participation in government when in office and of social leadership when out of office. Herein lies the central theme of Confucian teaching, as Professor Bodde pointed out in *China's Cultural Tradition:*

. . . for central to Confucianism from the very beginning was an idea of key importance: that government is too vital a matter to be left solely to accidents of birth, and therefore requires that the hereditary nobles be assisted and advised in their rule by an elite body of officials who are educationally qualified for their important task. This education, furthermore, should be broadly humanistic and ethical rather than narrowly technical.[15]

11 *The Book of Change.*
12 *The Analects.*
13 *Ibid.*
14 *Mencius.*
15 Derk Bodde, *China's Cultural Tradition* (New York: Rinehart and Co., 1957), p. 51.

There was thus the central idea of government by moral example. An educated man, by virtue of his superior morality, was entitled to rule without having to acquire specific and technical knowledge. In fact, such technical matters as taxation, settlement of lawsuits, water conservation, and even frontier defense, were for the most part left in the hands of a small group of specialists commonly designated as *Li* or clerks who, although educated in the ordinary sense of the term, were not regarded as scholars. On the other hand, there was a firm belief in what might be called the omniscience of the scholar who presumably was capable of finding solutions for practically all kinds of human problems, including the successful conduct of warfare.

The vital role of the scholars in the traditional Chinese state earned for the educated elite the common designation of scholar-officials. In a social context, the same group was known as the scholar-gentry, about whom Professor Michael wrote:

The gentry of imperial China were a distinct social group. They had recognized political, economic, and social privileges and powers and led a special mode of life. The gentry stood above the large mass of commoners and the so-called mean people. They dominated the social and economic life of Chinese communities and were also the stratum from which the officials came.[16]

Members of the scholar-gentry were leaders of traditional Chinese society in all important aspects of national life. They were, first of all, the custodians of China's cultural heritage, the transmitters and promoters of Confucian teaching. They were also civic leaders in all major fields of activity, including the preservation of peace, protection against bandits, construction and maintenance of public works, and mediation between the government and the populace at large. The status of gentry, however, was a legal one and theoretically could only be achieved through a series of examinations given by the

16 Franz Michael's Introduction in C. L. Chang, *The Chinese Gentry* (Seattle, Wash.: University of Washington Press, 1955), p. xiii.

state, although at times of decline of dynastic power and financial resources, other avenues were made available for entry into this elite group.

## THE TRADITIONAL SYSTEM OF EDUCATION AND IMPERIAL EXAMINATIONS

It is, of course, exceedingly difficult to speak of a system of education in traditional China when the term traditional implies the long span that preceded the modern period, and when changes and modifications were made to suit the needs of different periods of time. However, some general observations can be made concerning the characteristics of traditional Chinese education. One is the unique phenomenon of a formalized system of examinations which formed an integral part of the educational system, designed primarily for the *selection* rather than the education of the Chinese elite. Second, there existed a dual system of education comprising private and state sectors, with the former assuming greater significance as time went on. Third, in a qualitative sense, the content of traditional education has always been exclusively humanistic and classical in nature and was, generally speaking, divorced from practical considerations. And last, there was a noticeable trend toward inflexibility and formalism, due principally to overemphasis on the examinations, which resulted in the stultification of the spirit of free inquiry.

As it existed in the early part of the nineteenth century, on the eve of the penetration of Western influence into China, the state school system, if indeed it could be called a system, consisted of a number of educational institutions located in administrative centers of the Chinese Empire, mostly in county seats and prefectures, to which scholars aspiring to higher degrees would go for lectures by government educational officials. They were given examinations at regular intervals and records were kept on their progress. In the capital city of the Empire was the Imperial Academy, regarded as the highest institution of learning, but in actuality less an institution

of learning than part of the colossal imperial bureau-
cratic apparatus. Admission into the Academy meant no
more than the acquisition of a title for the student, and
residence was not required.

Strictly speaking, the government merely provided
educational centers run by supervisory personnel charged
with the responsibility of selecting persons for government service. As a consequence, the education of the
young was left to private institutions, which varied according to geography and economic resources. The private schools can be classified as follows: (1) family schools,
found exclusively in official and gentry families which
were sufficiently wealthy to hire a tutor for the young;
(2) clan schools, operated and financed by clans, to
which youngsters of the clan were admitted, usually under the tutelage of an elder member of the clan considered qualified to give instructions; (3) village schools,
organized and sponsored by leading families in the village where fees were charged according to the financial
abilities of the parents; and (4) private academies, located in large cities or places of exceptional natural
beauty, where nationally known scholars attracted a
group of students for high-level academic work on a
voluntary basis.

With the exception of the private academies, which
served as true centers of learning and as such performed
an invaluable function in the perpetuation of China's
scholarly tradition, the other types of schools, by and
large, were concerned with training and preparing the
young for the imperial examinations. In terms of quality
and academic standard, the family schools, by virtue of
their exclusive character and ability to attract teachers
of superior quality, ranked above the clan schools, while
the village schools invariably occupied the lowest position. The socioeconomic implication of such an educational arrangement is not difficult to see. Despite the
Confucian belief in the equality of educational opportunities, the scholar-gentry class enjoyed a clear advantage over the commoners, who educated their young at
considerable sacrifices because of the expenditures in-

volved and the loss of labor which might otherwise have been available. This, together with the less tangible cultural and environmental advantages, tended to make the scholar-gentry class self-perpetuating and to separate its members from the rest of the population.

From very early days, the selection of able and promising scholars for participation in government was considered an essential function of the Chinese state. The institutions designed for this purpose varied from dynasty to dynasty, but from the T'ang dynasty (618–906) on, the imperial examination system remained the principal avenue leading to officialdom, until its abolition in 1905. As it existed in the nineteenth century, the system consisted of a series of government-sponsored examinations, beginning with those given in the *hsien* or counties, which formed the basic administrative units of the Chinese Empire. Students with proper training could apply for admission to these examinations, provided they were certified by government-appointed guarantors as to their family background.[17] The county examinations were followed by a series of examinations on the prefecture level, under the supervision of the provincial Educational Commissioner who traveled from one area to another within the province at regular intervals. Those who succeeded in passing these examinations were given the degree of licentiate, the Chinese term for this degree being *Sheng-yuan,* commonly called *Hsiu-ts'ai,* or budding talent. Holders of this degree and others with equivalent qualifications were permitted to take the provincial examination, held once every three years in the provincial capital, under the supervision of a government examiner and his deputies appointed by the central government. In the more populous regions of the Empire, participants on this level often numbered in the tens of thousands, while the quota of successful candidates remained in the hundreds. Those fortunate enough to pass were awarded the degree of provincial

17 Theoretically examinations were open to all except those from families of socially undesirable occupations such as entertainers, operators of houses of ill-repute, and the like.

graduate, the Chinese title being *Chu-jen,* or elevated man.

Beyond the provincial level, there was the metropolitan examination, held in the nation's capital triennially, in which only candidates with the provincial graduate's degree and equivalent qualifications were permitted to take part. Equally competitive, only a fraction of the participants would pass and receive the degree of metropolitan graduate, the Chinese title being *Chin-shih,* or advanced scholar. There was also the institution known as the palace examination, theoretically held in the presence of the Emperor, as the final phase of the metropolitan examination. Those who passed with honors were appointed to the Han-lin Academy, the highest institution of learning in the Chinese Empire.[18]

This elaborate arrangement operated within an exceedingly complex civil service system, entrance into which was, at least in theory, a prerogative reserved for the successful candidates, although in practice this may not have been the case. However, even though the earning of a degree did not mean automatic entry into officialdom, it meant the acquisition of state-prescribed legal privileges. The extent of such privileges varied according to the level of achievement and in general was reflected in socioeconomic terms, such as exemption from *corvée,* special consideration in legal litigations, mode of transportation, and even the style and material of clothing. Extralegal privileges also existed in many different forms and were often abused to such a degree as to cause serious social malcontent and popular disaffection. As suggested earlier, the Chinese state from time to time resorted to means other than examinations to recruit members of the officialdom and to bestow honors and privileges on individuals. By and large, deviation from the normal procedure occurred more frequently during

18 This description of the examination system is of necessity greatly simplified, the system itself being exceedingly elaborate and complex. For further details, see first chapter by Han Yu-shan in H. F. MacNair, ed., *China* (Berkeley, Calif.: University of California Press, 1946).

periods of dynastic decline, but even then those members of the scholar-official class who had come up the hard way enjoyed the distinct designation of "having traveled the regular road," and as such commanded greater respect.

In addition to being the major avenue to social and political advancement, the examinations served the purpose of preserving the Confucian orthodoxy which in its turn justified the social structure. The profound concern with Confucian orthodoxy manifested itself in the state's emphasis on mastery of the Confucian classics as the sole criterion for judging scholarship, although different schools of interpretation gained ascendancy at different times. From the fourteenth century on, both the form and substance of the imperial examinations tended to become more rigid and formalistic, with the result that, by the nineteenth century, examination essay writing had developed into a fine art, divorced from the ethical principles—the basis of Confucian orthodoxy. As a consequence, scholars throughout the empire were concerned first of all with the acquisition of degrees rather than with learning.[19] Absurdities of all kinds, including misreading of the Confucian texts, arbitrary and illogical punctuation, and ludicrous allusions, became commonplace.

A critical re-examination of traditional Chinese education and its concomitant examinations leads to a few general observations. In the first place, traditional education was carried on under the enormous weight of orthodoxy and traditionalism, the whole process of learning being oriented toward the ideals of antiquity. The concept of progress was almost nonexistent, and even reforms of the mildest nature had to be proposed in the context as well as under the pretext of restoring the perfect order of the remote past. Thus both in institution

19 Beginning with the Ming Dynasty, the style of examination essay was popularly known as the Eight-legged essay, which stressed symmetry and stylistic formalism. See Shang Yen-liu, *Ch'ing-tai K'o-chü K'ao-shih shu-lu* (A General Account of the Civil Service Examination System of the Ch'ing Dynasty) (Peking: San Lien Book Co., 1958), chap. 7.

and content, traditional Chinese education was concerned more with the selection of the elite than with the education of the people. In the second place, excessive veneration of antiquity inescapably resulted in the stultification of thinking and was reflected in the tremendous emphasis placed on memorization and imitation of the classics as the sole means of pedagogy. The Chinese phrase "reading books" became synonymous with "search for knowledge," while the common appellation of a "scholar" became simply "a man who reads books." Finally, the idea of practicality was patently absent in traditional Chinese education; as a matter of fact, for a person to be concerned with matters of practical or utilitarian value was to disqualify himself for identification with the "book-reading" elite, hence the proverbial long fingernails of traditional scholars and the peculiar usage of the word scholar to mean "uselessness."

If the foregoing observations tend to be critical of education in traditional China, one must hasten to add that, within the cultural context and the value system then prevailing, this form of education served the needs of the nation remarkably well, and the characteristics of cultural continuity and stability were largely attributable to it. Ideologically, the stress on the Confucian doctrines of humanness, moderation, social harmony, and moral perfection had the effect of providing a noble yet attainable goal of life for the Chinese nation for centuries, and the truly lasting and inspiring aspects of Chinese civilization were fundamentally expressions of such Confucian ideals.[20] Politically, the theory and practice of selecting the best educated for government service, despite periods of chaos and internal turmoil, were responsible for the effective government and cultural development so characteristic of traditional China, in the positive sense, and for restraining excesses and abuses inherent in an autocracy, in the negative sense. Socially, the education and examination systems helped to ensure a basi-

[20] Wang Feng-chieh, *Chung-kuo chiao-yu shih* (History of Chinese Education), rev. ed. (Taipei: Cheng Chung Book Co., 1958), pp. 265 ff.

cally open society and to prevent the emergence of a hereditary aristocracy. For an agrarian economy striving for self-sufficiency, the lack of educational concern with economic and related practical problems becomes readily understandable. In a word, traditional Chinese education was a product of traditional Chinese culture and society as well as a major force sustaining that culture and society.

## THE MODERNIZATION OF CHINESE EDUCATION

Being extremely proud of their civilization, the Chinese had long regarded themselves as the custodians of human wisdom and their land as the center of the civilized world. Within the East Asian context, the Chinese Empire waxed and waned as the cyclical pattern of Chinese history unfolded, but at no time was China's cultural superiority so challenged as to necessitate fundamental change. The intensification of Western impact in the early part of the nineteenth century, however, heralded not only the end of a long-established order but also the beginning of a century of humiliation and agonizing readjustment. In an extraordinarily brief period of time, virtually all aspects of Chinese culture and all phases of Chinese life were subjected to the irresistable onslaught of the West. Beginning in the early 1840's, China yielded steadily in the face of the advancing Western powers until it was, by the end of the last century, reduced to the status of a semicolony. The modernization of Chinese education took place in this historical context; it grew in dimension and intensity in response to the impact of the West, not as a result of the spontaneous working of indigenous forces.

The modernization of Chinese education proceeded along Western lines. It formed one part of the larger cultural transformation of China known as Westernization. Broadly speaking, the entire process can be conveniently divided into three periods. The first lasted from 1862 to 1901; the second, from 1902 to 1921; and the third, from 1922 to 1949, when the Communist regime ascended to power. Inasmuch as this volume is primarily concerned with education under Communism, the modernization phase will be treated as a transition period, and therefore only briefly discussed.

The year 1862 marked the establishment of separate schools which deviated greatly from the traditional, both in organization and in content. Until 1901, this period was characterized by the gradual increase in the number of individual educational institutions, each established for a specific purpose, but all having the common object of better preparing China for coping with the Western powers. For the nation as a whole, the traditional pattern persisted, and the modern schools existed in addition to, rather than as substitutions for, the traditional schools. The nature of these schools and the sequence in which they appeared on the Chinese educational scene were indicative of the national needs as seen and understood by the ruling group of the time.

In their order of appearance, the new schools fell into three categories: language training institutes, technical schools, and military academies. The first foreign language institute, designed to train diplomatic personnel through the teaching of foreign languages, was founded in 1862 in the capital city of Peking; later such technical subjects as mathematics and astronomy were added to its curriculum. In 1866, the first technical school was established in Fukien, in this instance a maritime school where shipbuilding and navigation were the major subjects. This and later attempts at developing an industrial potential was China's educational response to the Western challenge, recognizing that Western superiority came from the mastery of modern technology. In 1881, the first naval academy came into existence in Tientsin, an event that signified the acceleration of China's Westernization.

When measured against the objectives for which such educational efforts were made, namely the strengthening of China and meeting the challenge of the foreign "barbarians," this early phase of educational reform was far from successful for the simple reason that the schools were

only isolated and half-hearted attempts at modernization, without the necessary resources, planning, determination, and, indeed, sufficient understanding, to make
them work. At the same time, it must be pointed out
that though faltering, these were steps in the right direction, and the impact on educational thinking and intellectual climate was both real and profound.

The second phase of transition began in 1902 when,
having suffered a crushing defeat in the Sino-Japanese
War of 1894–1895, and realizing the inadequacy of partial efforts, the Chinese government adopted a new and
elaborate system of education which called for the establishment of modernized schools on all levels. The truly
significant aspect of educational development during this
period was, however, not so much the institutional
changes brought about by government action as a fundamental shift in the formulation of educational policy.
If, during the first period, the Chinese had hoped to resist Western encroachment by adopting certain Western
methods but preserving its traditional culture and institutions, after 1902 it became increasingly clear that more
thorough and radical educational measures were necessary for national survival. The abolition of the ancient
and time-honored examination system in 1905 was an
eloquent example of the extent of the changes which
had occurred.

No educational change, however, can take place in a
vacuum or be completely independent of the larger social forces at work. While the adoption of a new education system in 1902, reinforced by a more forward-look-
ing approach to education, represented a further step
toward modernization, the over-all political, economic,
and social conditions of China in the last days of imperial rule were such that implementation of the new
education plan proved to be beyond the capacity of the
state. Continued chaos in the early republican era likewise impeded the healthy development of education,
and the elaborate system of schools remained largely on
paper.

Despite the utterly chaotic conditions manifest in the

decline of dynastic power, economic dislocation, and social unrest, a foundation was nevertheless being laid for
the further development of education along Western
lines. Ironically, achievements on the educational front
were due more to the inability of the state to assume direct control over education than to the limited efforts
made by the state. Moreover, educational achievements
of a genuine and lasting nature during this period generally had the effect of working against, rather than for,
the preservation of the *status quo*.

The outstanding feature during this phase of modernization in Chinese education was the steady broadening
of the horizons of the Chinese intelligentsia, resulting in
the unhesitating acceptance of Western ideas and the
abandonment of Chinese traditions. Several factors contributed to this phenomenon. In the first place, the increasing number of Chinese returning from study abroad,
with rare exceptions, became advocates for all-out Westernization and agents of cultural change.[21] Second, with
the introduction of a new education system, new institutions of secondary and higher education came into existence in major centers all over China. Though small in
number, their intellectual and educational influence was
out of all proportion. Third, with the expansion of Western powers, the number of schools under foreign missionary auspices steadily increased, with more and more
Chinese exposed directly to Western teaching.[22] Finally,
the abolition of the examination system rendered the traditional type of schools obsolete, since traditional education no longer provided an avenue to social and political
advancement. The conservative traditionalists, who had
been identified with the old system of education, also lost
ground on the intellectual front. Consequently, not only
did the number of old schools diminish but Confucian orthodoxy itself, for which they stood, was shaken to its
foundation.

21 The sending of Chinese students to Europe and America began
in 1868. After the Sino-Japanese War, more went to Japan.
22 American religious organizations played a very important role
in the extension of Western knowledge to China. The earliest American school was founded in 1845 in Shanghai.

The third period of transition began in 1922 when a still newer system of education was adopted. The battle against traditional education having been won, this period was marked by a stabilization and rationalization of education, particularly after 1927 when the establishment of the national government in Nanking brought warlordism and disunity to an end. Without going into details, educational development during this period followed certain notable trends. There was, first of all, the tendency toward professional guidance in education. Whereas in the past the belief persisted that any "book-reading" scholar was capable of directing educational affairs, it now became clear that the formulation of fundamental educational policy required the services of specially trained educationists. Second, within the framework of professionalization, a noticeable shift in educational leadership took place during this period, a shift from a Japan-oriented leadership to one that was United States–oriented. This shift not only affected the composition of the leadership group but also resulted in a basic change in educational philosophy. Organizations such as the National Association for the Advancement of Education, of which American-trained educators formed the nucleus, advocated structural changes after the American model, favored a diversified curriculum, and declared as the central objectives of education the development of sound personality and the promotion of democratic spirit. Third, with the stabilization of Nationalist rule, the process of rationalization began and Western ideas and practices in education were adapted to national needs. Increasing emphasis on science and technology, introduction of military training, establishment of separate vocational and teacher preparation institutions were concrete examples of some of the efforts in that direction.

Actually, the entire period of transition may be studied from a quite different angle, taking into consideration those crucial historical events which impinged on modern educational thought.

China's defeat in the Opium War of 1839–1842, crushing as it was, did not produce an immediate awakening on the part of the Chinese scholar-officials. It was not until the capture of Peking by the Anglo-French forces in 1860 that *self-strengthening* began in earnest. The educational part of this movement started with foreign language teaching, mentioned above, and later extended to other efforts collectively known as "Western Learning," an educational movement that was subjected to different interpretations but in general tended to regard as necessary subjects those branches of learning absent in traditional China. Because of the pressing need for national defense, another school advocated technical education, holding the belief that the mastery of Western technology would bring about national salvation while leaving intact the substance of Chinese culture. Educational efforts in this direction included the military schools, maritime schools, and similar enterprises. However, the defeat at the hands of the Japanese in 1895 convinced many Chinese leaders that mere imitation of Western technical education was not sufficient, hence began the movement in favor of education in Western political ideas and institutions, the underlying objectives being the modernization of government structure on Western and Japanese models. The Hundred Day Reform of 1898, despite its failure, indicated the extent to which the concept of modern education had broadened with the deepening of national crisis.

The founding of the Chinese Republic in 1912 brought two thousand years of autocracy to an end. In the wake of the Republican revolution, three new schools of educational thought emerged, emphasizing utilitarianism, aesthetics, and vocational education. The first advocated education for concrete utilitarian purposes and was clearly concerned with the economic development of China at a time when the very foundation of Chinese economy was undermined by Western penetration. Aesthetics education, to which Ts'ai Yuan-p'ei, one of the greatest Republican educators, devoted his efforts, sought to provide a new humanistic approach to education, a substitute for the now discredited Confucian system of ethics. As for vocational education, it was first and fore-most a reaction against the bookishness and impractical-ity of the older times, seeking to lift the society out of apathy and inaction through the preparation of voca-tionally capable citizens. All three schools had their sup-porters, and experiments were carried on in different parts of the country, simultaneously, and independent of one another.

Toward the end of the second decade of the twentieth century, the numerically small but intellectually influen-tial group of intelligentsia, now the products of modern education, had come of age. Their dissatisfaction with affairs of state reached the exploding point in 1919 when their demonstration against the government found na-tionwide sympathy and response in such an overpower-ing manner that the May Fourth Movement of that year became an important landmark in modern Chinese his-tory. From then on, those who stressed scientific educa-tion and mass education dominated the scene. The visits to China of John Dewey, and later of Paul Monroe and others, were part of the movement which sought to cre-ate a scientific basis for education. "Mr. Science" and "Mr. Democracy" became the guiding lights of the day, and under the banner of democracy mass education found its eager sponsors in such world-renowned men as James Yen. It was clear that, notwithstanding the difficulties in which China found herself, the educational front steadily moved closer to what the Chinese thinkers believed was the true core of Western culture and, instead of search-ing for temporary and partial solutions, there was now a demand for total Westernization.

The consolidation of Nationalist rule after 1928 ush-ered in still another era during which the implementa-tion of Sun Yat-sen's "Three People's Principles" was de-clared to be the fundamental task of education. Civic training, social education, rural education, labor service, and military training were some of the means employed by the state. After 1931, as Japanese aggression intensi-fied, national survival became the major concern of edu-cation. The outbreak of hostilities in 1937 plunged China into eight long years of bitter struggle which resulted in the curtailment of civil liberties, increasing interference by the Kuomintang in educational affairs, and steady deterioration of social and economic conditions. Thus the war not only arrested the forward movement evident in the pre-war days but also alienated an increasingly large number of intellectuals.

The three periods, which together saw the complete transformation of Chinese education along modern lines, corresponded to the three stages of China's response to the West: periods of resistance, compromise, and acceptance. Underlying all three was the central theme of adjusting to the demands of a modern world in which the West dominated. In retrospect, educational reforms in modern China have always come too late and been too little, and the fortunes of China as a nation have suffered despite educational efforts. The ascendancy of Western-trained intellectuals has meant the popularization of certain key Western concepts such as liberalism, democracy, individualism, and a scientific approach to problems of life, but this was largely among the educated who constituted only a fraction of the Chinese populace. At the same time, rejection of the traditional Confucian orthodoxy gave rise to cultural dislocation, aggravated by the inability of Western-oriented intellectuals to agree as to the means for achieving Western ideals. Without intending to be harsh, the point can be made that the painful process of modernization of Chinese education produced only a small group of individualistic specialists, who were removed from the masses and unable to exercise sufficient influence on either politics or society, and thus "materially diminished the chance of democracy in China and promoted, by default, the opposite cause." [23]

## CHINESE EDUCATION UNDER COMMUNISM

Paradoxically, the contemporary phase of China's development under Communism is at once an extreme form

23 Y. C. Wang, "Intellectuals and Society in China, 1860–1949," *Comparative Studies in Society and History*, vol. III, no. 4, July, 1961, p. 426.

**SCHOOL SYSTEM IN COMMUNIST CHINA, 1958**

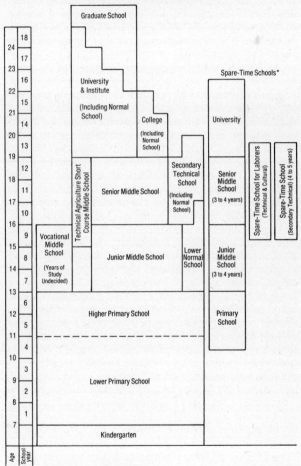

*Age level does not apply to Spare-Time Schools.

25

of Westernization and a partial reversion to traditional patterns. The totalitarian character of the present regime is not only reminiscent of the ancient autocratic order, but its acceptance may be attributed to the acquiescense engendered by that tradition. On the ideological front, the state of confusion of thought, compounded by almost a century's cultural dislocation, has been brought to an abrupt end with the promulgation of Marxism-Leninism as the state ideology which, though antithetic to Confucian orthodoxy in every essential way, is equally pervasive. Inasmuch as the ideological reconditioning of the Chinese nation is first and foremost an educational task, education has become the exclusive concern of the Communist state. Moreover, within the Marxian ideological framework, the pursuit of concrete national goals requires the education of the Chinese people. Hence there are two major aspects in the study of Chinese education under Communism: fundamental principles and actual implementation—in short, theory and practice.

There is, strictly speaking, very little in the Chinese Communist educational literature that can be regarded as educational theory per se. What the Chinese Communists have labeled educational theory is no more than the extension and application of certain aspects of dialectical materialism, as expounded by Marx, Lenin, Stalin, and Mao, to the direction of educational affairs. Since Communist doctrine stresses the unity of theory and practice, as well as the importance of "concrete objective conditions," any educational policy or measure can be introduced and promoted or criticized and abandoned in the name of either theory or practice.

## THE IDEOLOGICAL BASIS: THE FIRST TRIAD

Of particular significance and relevance to education are three basic concepts of dialectical materialism as interpreted by the Chinese Communists. The first is the classification of human thought, insofar as the laws of the development of the world are concerned, into the metaphysical and the dialectical which represent two mutually opposed world outlooks. Mao Tse-tung wrote in his "On Contradiction":

For a very long period of history both in China and in Europe, metaphysics formed part of the idealist world outlook and occupied a dominant position in human thought. In the early days of the bourgeoisie in Europe, materialism was also metaphysical. The Marxist materialist-dialectical world outlook emerged because in many European countries social economy had entered the stage of highly developed capitalism, the productive forces, the class struggle and the sciences had all developed to a level unprecedented in history, and the industrial proletariat had become the greatest motive force in historical development. Then among the bourgeoisie, besides an openly avowed, extremely barefaced reactionary idealism, there also emerged vulgar evolutionism to oppose materialist dialectics.[24]

In this short passage one comes across a number of the familiar Communist terms: class struggle, bourgeoisie, proletariat, productive forces, capitalism, reactionary idealism, and materialist dialectics. No useful purpose can be served by raising philosophical questions about any one of these terms, nor is it relevant to ask if the majority of the Communist followers understand the meaning and implications of these terms. It is, however, exceedingly important to bear in mind that, by categorizing all human thought according to such a scheme, a simple formula now exists by which all thinking and action can be judged. The *metaphysical* world outlook is equated with idealism, is adhered to by the bourgeoisie, is reactionary, and therefore is opposed to both human progress and scientific truth. On the opposite side is the *dialectical* world outlook which is founded on objective scientific truth, represents the irresistible forward-running current of history, is supported by the proletariat, and promises the Communist millennium. Thus the line between right and wrong, friend and enemy, progress and reaction is irrevocably drawn, with the party leadership enjoying the exclusive prerogative of interpretation. Ideological rigidity forbids deviation in thought, yet allows

24 Mao Tse-tung, "On Contradiction," in *Selected Works of Mao Tse-tung* (London: Lawrence and Wishart Ltd., 1954), vol. 2, p. 14.

sufficient tactical latitude for the party itself. The state of confusion of thought in modern China has been brought to an end; education now proceeds in an atmosphere of controlled uniformity.

The second concept concerns practice, with even greater and more direct implications for education. To quote Mao Tse-tung once more:

> Knowledge starts with practice, reaches the theoretical plane via practice, and then has to return to practice. The active function of knowledge not only manifests itself in the active leap from perceptual knowledge to rational knowledge, but also—and this is the more important—in the leap from rational knowledge to revolutionary practice. The knowledge which enables us to grasp the laws of the world must be redirected to the practice of changing the world, that is, it must again be applied in the practice of production, in the practice of the revolutionary class struggle and revolutionary national struggle, as well as in the practice of scientific experimentation. This is the process of testing and developing theory, the continuation of the whole process of knowledge.[25]

The nature of knowledge is thus defined. Since search for knowledge is the prime objective of education, any form of education that fails to attain knowledge through practice according to the prescribed formula of production, class struggle, and national struggle is worse than no education at all. If, by classifying human thoughts into two fundamental opposing world views in favor of the dialectical, the Communists seek to create a monolithic pattern of ideological conformity, this emphasis on practice tends to determine both the nature of knowledge and the meaning of education. Ideologically, the Chinese educational tradition can thus be negated on the ground that it was divorced from practice, hence its failure to lift China out of primitive agrarianism, to eliminate class exploitation, to achieve national power, and to reap the benefits of modern science. The feverish action-oriented form of education in China today can be understood only in terms of this fundamental consideration.

The third part of the triad is the class character of education and culture in general. Culture and education

25 Mao Tse-tung, "On Practice," *Ibid.*, vol. 2, pp. 292–293.

are regarded as concrete expressions of the politics and economics of a given society, and the politics and economics are determined by the class character. With respect to China, Mao Tse-tung's analysis of the problem of culture begins with an interpretation of China's culture before the Communist revolution, which he describes in the following terms:

There is in China an imperialist culture which is a reflection of the control or partial control of imperialism over China politically and economically. This form of culture is advocated not only by the cultural organizations run directly by the imperialists in China but also by a number of shameless Chinese. All culture that contains a slave ideology belongs to this category. There is also in China a semi-feudal culture which is a reflection of semi-feudal politics and economy and has as its representatives all those who, while opposing the new culture and new ideologies, advocate the worship of Confucius, the study of the Confucian canon, the old ethical code and the old ideologies. Imperialist culture and semi-feudal culture are affectionate brothers, who have formed a reactionary cultural alliance to oppose China's new culture. This reactionary culture serves the imperialists and the feudal class, and must be swept away.26

The "reactionary culture" must be condemned and swept away because it served only the interests of the exploiting classes which were allied with imperialism and semifeudalism. This forms the negative aspect of Mao's interpretation. In a positive sense, Mao advocated the "new democratic culture which can only be led by the proletarian cultural ideology, by the ideology of communism, and cannot be led by the cultural ideology of any other class." 27 It is, in a word, the culture of the broad masses under the leadership of the proletariat.

## THE FUNDAMENTAL PRINCIPLES: THE SECOND TRIAD

Although there have been tactical retreats on the educational front since the Communist takeover, the three

26 Mao-Tse-tung, "On New Democracy," *Ibid.*, vol. 3, p. 141.
27 *Ibid.*, p. 145.

fundamental concepts concerning the dialectical world outlook, the search for true knowledge through practice, and the development of a proletarian culture have remained the very foundation on which education rests. In this respect, there seems to be a remarkable degree of ideological consistency in the Communist regime, because the educational principles laid down in the Common Programme, which served as the basic guiding rules of the land until the adoption of a constitution in 1954, specifically called for the creation of a culture and education of the New Democracy, "that is, nationalistic, scientific, and popular." [28] These make up the second triad of nationalism, scientism, and popularism which, unlike the first which provides the ideological basis, sets up the educational objectives toward which the regime should strive. The achievement of these objectives requires action; now that the Communists are in power, they lose no time in remolding Chinese education according to the ideological dictates.

There can be little doubt that nationalism has been one of the most pervasive and dynamic forces in modern China, and the Communists have manipulated it to their fullest advantage. To achieve the nationalistic goal through education, two major strategies have been employed. On the positive side, the Chinese people are taught to cherish their great cultural tradition, and are reminded of the lasting achievements of their forefathers, the vastness and richness of their land, and the tremendous potentials for the betterment of mankind.[29] Negatively, the humiliation of the Chinese nation during the past century, the sufferings of the Chinese people, and the degradation of China to the status of a semicolony are ascribed to the unrelenting aggressions on all fronts

28 Article 41 of the Common Programme, adopted by the Chinese People's Political Consultative Conference which functioned as the highest law-making organ immediately after the Communist seizure of power in 1949. Chapter V of the Programme deals with culture and education.

29 See, for example, a collection of essays entitled *Lun ai-kuo chu-i ti chiao-yü* (Essays on Education for Patriotism), by Hsü T'e-li and others (Peking: The Mass Bookstore, 1951).

by the arrogant and vicious imperialists. If the "victory" of the Chinese people in freeing themselves has broken the political bondage of semicolonialism, the vestiges of imperialist culture and education still present the most serious obstacle to the achievement of the culture of the New Democracy.

It is for the "nationalistic" purpose that all Western-sponsored institutions of education were the first to be subjected to the fury of educational reorganization, and in less than three years, from early 1950 to the fall of 1952, all schools with foreign affiliations were "reorganized" out of existence.[30] Labeled as agencies of imperialist cultural aggression, the foreign-supported schools were declared hotbeds for the spread of individualism, liberalism, and bourgeois decadence, all implacable enemies of the culture of the New Democracy. Similarly, the Western-trained intellectuals, their repentence and profession of faith in the new order notwithstanding, were subjected to the severest forms of thought reform.[31]

The "scientific" part of the triad involves two directly related objectives. The first has to do with the acceptance of the Communist definition of knowledge, discussed above, which can be scientific only when it is dialectical and derived through practice. Within such an ideological framework, scientific education means specifically the development of modern science and technology to expedite the process of industrialization and national construction. Concrete educational efforts in this direction have been both numerous and concentrated, and fall under three general categories. On the highest level is the Chinese Academy of Sciences, which has steadily expanded over the past twelve years. The number of its research institutes increased from 31 in 1952 to 170 in 1958, with a corresponding increase in trained person-

[30] For further information on the fate of foreign-supported schools of higher education, see C. T. Hu, "Higher Education in Mainland China," in *Comparative Education Review*, vol. 4, no. 3, February 1961, p. 163.

[31] For a thorough and up-to-date analysis of the thought reform of intellectuals, see Theodore H. E. Chen, *Thought Reform of the Chinese Intellectuals* (Hongkong: University Press, 1960).

nel which in 1958 numbered some 30,000.[32] The Academy is responsible for the training of scientists, who form the nucleus of an expanding army of technical manpower. Below the Academy are the institutions of higher and secondary education, the majority of which are devoted to the training of engineers, technicians of all types, medical personnel, and other specialists. On the lowest level are the schools for the "broad masses of the people" who are taught not only reading and writing but also the rudiments of modern science and technology, consisting primarily, at the present stage, of labor-saving devices. Underlying the whole educational process is the principle of "walking on two legs," which demands the combination of theory and practice, new and old, Western and Chinese.

The idea of popularism has grown out of the concept of class struggle, and thereby differs fundamentally from its counterpart in non-Communist countries. Concerning the class structure of Chinese society, Mao Tse-tung as early as 1926 wrote an essay entitled "Analysis of the Classes in Chinese Society" in which he classified the Chinese population into three basically different social groups with respect to the Chinese revolution: those for it, those against it, and those wavering between the two.[33] Since the culture and education of China before the Communist revolution favored the oppressing classes, the culture and education of the New Democracy must serve the needs of the masses under the leadership of the proletariat. Needless to say, the Communists are fully aware of the educational needs of the nation at a time of all-out national construction which cannot be accomplished without a literate and technically competent populace. Therefore, from both the ideological viewpoint of class struggle and the practical viewpoint of the nation's educational needs, popularism in education must be held

---

[32] Leo A. Orleans, *Professional Manpower and Education in Communist China* (Washington, D.C.: National Science Foundation, 1960), p. 111.

[33] Mao Tse-tung, "Analysis of the Classes in Chinese Society," in *Selected Works of Mao Tse-tung, op. cit.,* vol. 1, pp. 13–20.

up as one of the major goals. The slogan "Intellectualize the proletariat; proletarianize the intellectuals!" reveals in a nutshell the true meaning of the movement toward popularism.

A variety of means have been employed to popularize education. Of first importance has been the steady expansion of numbers on all levels. Enrollment in full-time institutions is reported to have increased by leaps and bounds, with a corresponding increase in the number of schools. In 1958, the government claimed that 85 per cent of all school-age children were in attendance.[34] With the advent of the "Great Leap Forward" in that year, the informal part of education received encouragement and attention, resulting in the creation, sometimes almost overnight, of literally thousands of spare-time schools (see pages 38–39) and "Red-and-Expert" colleges. These schools are undoubtedly far below standard and in some cases exist merely in name; but they are indicative of the extent to which the goal of popularism has been sought. The class character of the students has also shifted in favor of the proletariat, which by Chinese definition includes both agricultural and industrial workers. According to official reports, the percentage of students of working-class origin increased from 19.1 per cent in 1951 to 48 per cent in 1958 for higher education, and from 51.3 per cent to 75.2 per cent in the secondary schools.[35] This is known as "opening the doors of schools for peasants and workers"—in other words, "the intellectualization of the proletariat." At the same time, the "proletarianization of the intellectuals" has proceeded according to party dictates, largely through thought reform, intensive indoctrination, and participation in productive labor. By and large, the quality of education in the present phase of development seems to have declined; that is, as a result of the heavy demands made on the stu-

---

34 A breakdown of the enrollment for 1958 gave 86,400,000 for elementary schools; 10,000,000 for all types of secondary schools; and 660,000 for higher institutions. See *Wei-ta ti shih-nien* (Ten Great Years) (Peking: People's Publishing House, 1959), p. 170.

35 *Ibid.*, p. 178.

dents, the Communists have been more successful in bringing down the intellectuals than in raising the proletariat.

The real meaning of popularism seems to lie in the emerging pattern of education in which the education of the masses, however imperfect and qualitatively dubious in the present stage of development, takes precedence over other endeavors. Adherence to popularism is creating a new generation of educated Chinese who are children of the common people, sharing their hardships and aspirations, and no longer apart or aloof. It also means that the regime has embarked on the gigantic educational task of eradicating illiteracy, conquering superstition, and disseminating elementary scientific knowledge among some six hundred million Chinese. At the same time, those who are receiving secondary and higher education, including future nuclear physicists, are constantly reminded of their debt to the "people," to whom they must forever remain faithful servants. If the earlier phase of modern Chinese education, which began about a century ago, created a group of intellectuals who shared little with their traditional predecessors in outlook and temperament, the present generation has gone even further in renouncing the educational heritage of the recent past. The concept of popularism has, in a word, changed the social meaning of education as well as the social status of the educated.

## FOUNDATIONS OF EDUCATIONAL POLICY: THE THIRD TRIAD

By 1958, the Communist Party and the Communist state under its control were sufficiently convinced of the "correctness" of the party line and satisfied with the progress along the road to socialism up to that point to launch an all-out and nationwide movement known as the "Great Leap Forward." As education formed an integral and important part of this national challenge, fundamental policy decisions concerning education were proclaimed jointly by the Chinese Communist Party and the

State Council on September 19, 1958. "The policy of the educational work of the Party," it was stated, "is to make education serve proletarian politics, and to combine education and productive labor. In order to carry out this policy, educational work must be led by the Party."[36] Thus there appeared yet another triad, namely, politics, production, and party control.

To the Communists, the term politics is all-inclusive in its implications. By proletarian politics is meant, therefore, the whole intricate process of establishing a new national policy based on the leadership of the proletariat, of which the Communist Party is the vanguard. Aware that the Communist millennium must be created by a people completely immersed in Communist ideology, the party leadership sees no alternative but to assign to politics the highest priority in all educational tasks. It is significant to note, in this connection, that the party organization in China has no educational department as such, and that all major decisions concerning education are made by the party hierarchy on the recommendations of the Department of Propaganda. Given the role of the party in the functioning of the Chinese state, the Ministry of Education is no more than an administrative organ through which party decisions are effected. The obvious implication is that education, insofar as the party is concerned, is primarily propaganda; the indoctrination of the population is its ultimate aim.

Ideological indoctrination is the essence of the political part of the triad, and takes precedence over all other aspects of education. Consequently all persons, and especially educational workers and students, are graded, selected, and treated according to their "political consciousness." Academic excellence is, to be sure, desirable and encouraged, but it must be accompanied by political reliability resulting from proper indoctrination. The term "Red and Expert," is in this sense particularly pertinent and revealing, for being Red is more important than being Expert, and the objective of education is to train a

36 Reported in *Jen-min jih-pao* (People's Daily), Peking, September 20, 1958.

new generation of ideologically trustworthy and technically competent Chinese.

References have been made to the ideological framework in connection with the first triad. Our concern here is with the means by which the political objectives of education are achieved. A variety of methods are in use, ranging from the simple technique of repeating slogans to the highly complex process of thought reform. Broadly speaking, however, these methods fall into two categories, the formal or doctrinal part and the informal or action part. According to the Communist scheme, each complements the other, thereby unifying theory and practice.

On the formal or doctrinal side are the political subjects of instruction which consist of Dialectical Materialism, Foundations of Marxism and Leninism, History of Chinese Revolution, Political Economy, and the like. The titles and the manner of presentation of the courses may vary from level to level and from institution to institution, but they are "musts" in all cases, whether in the People's University or in a rural spare-time school. Moreover, instruction is given, in most cases, by party cadres operating in educational institutions. Passive acceptance of the doctrines never suffices, and such devices as "Study Groups," "criticism and self-criticism," and "thought struggle sessions" are resorted to from time to time not only to prevent deviation but also to ensure complete and absolute belief in the new faith. The informal or active part of indoctrination takes many forms, mostly in organized political activities of one sort or another. Teachers and students have in the past twelve years engaged in several large-scale campaigns, beginning with the first land reform movement in 1950, followed by the Resist-America Aid-Korea movement in 1951, the Three-Anti and Five-Anti movements of 1952, the Blooming and Contending of 1957, the Great Leap Forward of 1958, and more recently the movement to increase agricultural production.[37] These are political activities of

37 The Three-anti campaign was directed against the three evils of corruption, waste, and bureaucracy; the objects of the Five-anti campaign are tax evasion, bribery, cheating in government contracts,

considerable duration and scope; there were also a large number of short-term activities, such as mass demonstrations against the French and British during the Suez crisis, and against Eisenhower's visit to the Far East in 1960.

At present, there is every indication that political indoctrination is receiving the utmost emphasis in all educational activities. The regime seems to be fully aware of the effect of such emphasis on the quality of education, but as long as the principle of making education serve the needs of proletarian politics is followed, political indoctrination will continue to receive the highest priority.

In an article entitled "The Great Revolution and Development in Our Country's Educational Task," the Chinese Minister of Education made the following statement concerning the position of politics in education:

The great revolution in education further solved the problem of the relationship between education on the one hand and politics on the other. The capitalist class hypocritically chanted "education for education's sake" and "leave the students out of politics." But we insist that education must be in the service of proletarian politics and that all undertakings must be combined with political thought, because only in this way can we train the type of personnel who are both red and expert. For this reason, we hold up as the soul of all school work the political education of Marxism-Leninism and the political task of the Party. Moreover, we have put into effect the guiding principle of "let politics be the commander-in-chief" in all fields of cultural and scientific education.[38]

Two lines of argument are generally used to justify the policy of combining education with production. One is the fundamental ideological consideration of the nature of knowledge and the importance of practice in the acquisition of knowledge. To engage in productive activities is to combine practice with theory, and thus to ac-

---

theft of economic intelligence, and stealing of national property. The term "blooming and contending" refers to another mass movement, begun in 1956, which bore the name "Let the Hundred Flowers Bloom and Let the Hundred Schools of Thought Contend."

[38] *Chien-kuo shih-nien* (Ten Years of National Construction) (Hongkong: Chi-wen Publishing Co., 1959).

quire true knowledge. Also, productive labor is believed to be the surest way to eliminate the class character of education. Through productive labor the socially aloof and ideologically unwholesome intellectuals are made mindful of the dignity and honor of physical work and are proletarianized in the process. The second argument relates to the acute need of the nation for the total mobilization of its human resources. An expanding army of students, particularly on the secondary and higher education levels, is an extremely important asset, since students will eventually contribute far more to national development than unskilled workers. For economic as well as ideological reasons, therefore, the school system itself has been adjusted in such a way as to facilitate the combination of education with productive labor.

Within this context, there are now three major types of schools in China, namely, the spare-time schools, half-work half-study schools, and full-time schools. The spare-time schools are designed to elevate the cultural level and technical competence of the masses, and are, as the name itself indicates, organizationally flexible. Drawing students from the rural communes, industrial plants, and urban residential districts, these schools range from open-air literacy classes to technical training on farms and in factories. Since all participants, including instructional staff, have their regular tasks to perform, these schools represent a form of mass education in which production comes before education. Because the state has encouraged local authorities to assume major responsibility for the organization and operation of spare-time schools, and because of the diversity in objectives, resources, background of students, and other factors, there are no established patterns or criteria by which the spare-time schools can be properly described or classified. The schools themselves, however, are beset by common problems in both the mental and the physical realms. Overemphasis on political indoctrination in spare-time school instruction, often given in addition to regular political meetings of one form or another, has given rise to mental dissipation or resentment, while the compulsory nature of such schools has contributed to physical exhaustion, the working hours being long and arduous.

In the half-work half-study schools students are required to participate in active production in a large variety of fields on a half-day, half-week, or sometimes half-month basis. Both in organization and in curriculum these schools display a higher degree of articulation and coordination than the spare-time schools. In many cases they are middle schools under the supervision of government agencies. These agencies arrange with industrial or technical institutions to provide technical training and guidance for the students; in exchange the regular working force receives school instruction while the students are at work. Here education and production receive equal attention.

The full-time schools form the backbone of the nation's school system. Subject to the over-all control and supervision of the state in matters relating to organization, administration, finance, curriculum, admission, graduation, and assignment of work, they combine education with production, employing different means on different levels of instruction. For children below the secondary level, stress is laid on the cultivation of the correct attitude toward work. Whenever feasible, children are encouraged to perform manual labor in school, not so much for production as to prepare them for participation in "socialist construction." On the secondary and higher education levels, production becomes an integral part of education, and in this case covers a wide range of activities. University students majoring in Chinese language and literature compile dictionaries; geology students explore parts of the country for minerals; and students in economics or banking work in state-operated enterprises. Engineering institutes not only train their students in laboratory plants; they fulfill production quotas assigned by the state. The following statement illustrates the extent to which education has been combined with productive labor:

Labor has become a formal part of our school curriculum. Schools everywhere have established factories and farms. According to statistics submitted by 323 institutions of higher education, there are now 738 factories and 233 farms, the latter having a total cultivated area of 140,000 *mou* of land. During 1958 and 1959, 386,000 students put in altogether 36,460,-000 working days, with a total output valued at 1,380,000,000 *yuan*. All that we have belongs to the Party.[39]

It is idle to speculate on the effect of politics and productive labor on education, although it is generally known that there is deep-seated dissatisfaction with the present state of educational affairs. Inasmuch as there is public skepticism, the third cardinal policy calling for party control of education is indeed a necessity, for without it other educational goals would be impossible of achievement. The reaffirmation of this policy by no less a personage than Mao Tse-tung himself in 1958 is, therefore, not merely a reiteration of a familiar tune or theme, but an authoritative statement of the official party position concerning education, a position that tolerates no interference from other quarters.

The timing of this reaffirmation of party leadership in education is significant. It coincided with the "Great Leap Forward" and signaled the end of the earlier policy of tolerating to a certain degree the so-called old intelligentsia and allowing them a limited role in formulating educational policies. With the reaffirmation of this policy, all criticisms directed against various aspects of Chinese education were silenced and positive measures were taken to ensure complete and unquestioning implementation of party directives on education. These measures include intensified party work among the students, the strengthening of the power and authority of party representatives in schools, and the control of academic and administrative affairs by the state through the party apparatus. In August 1959, one newspaper reported that among the 60,000 or more graduates from institutions of higher education in 1959, the number of Party and Communist Youth League members reached a record high, with the Peking Normal University claiming as large a

39 A report by the Chairman of the All-China Students Union, *Hongkong Times*, February 11, 1960.

proportion as 85 per cent.[40] In virtually all schools, the party secretary, with the party machinery functioning at the lowest level, now wields absolute power over the essential aspects of school life, ranging from curriculum making to examination procedures to student selection.

A delegate to the All-China Conference of Advanced Socialist Workers in Education, Culture, Health, Physical Education, and Press, held in Peking in the summer of 1960, made the following statement concerning Party leadership:

The educational and cultural task of our country is a task of socialism. It is an instrument for the consolidation of proletariat dictatorship, and it is at the same time an instrument for the Communist education of our people. The fundamental principle is that education and cultural work must serve proletarian politics and socialist economic construction. In order to accomplish this, education must be led by our Party. Within the realm of education and culture, the struggle between the bourgeoisie and the proletariat and the struggle between capitalism and socialism have manifested themselves in many forms. Over a long time, the focus of contention has always been centered on the fundamental problem of Party leadership. Prior to 1957, despite the fact that we had made great gains in educational and cultural work, we were not able to consolidate, in time, the leadership of the proletariat. As a result, the bourgeois rightists, taking advantage of this condition, began to challenge the Party on all fronts, shouting such slogans as "The Party is incapable of leading educational work," "Education for education's sake," and "Separate labor from mental work." . . . The thorough crushing of the vicious attacks by the bourgeois rightists has firmly established the indisputable correctness of our Party's educational and cultural policy, has paved the way for even greater progress, and has made possible the Great Leap Forward on all fronts.[41]

## CONCLUSION

The revolt against tradition and the fundamental remaking of modern Chinese education form one impor-

[40] *Kuang-ming Daily*, August 24, 1959.
[41] *People's Daily*, June 2, 1960.

tant aspect of the transformation of the most populous nation on earth. The traditional educational system, like all other facets of Chinese national life, proved totally inadequate in the face of an unprecedented challenge from the West. With the abandonment of traditional education came the weakening, and later the disintegration, of the ideological, moral, and political fabric of old China. It took almost a century for Chinese education to develop to its present stage, a century of tortuous soul-searching, punctuated by moments of bold optimism and helpless frustration. In the earlier phase of the transitional period, when there still existed a semblance of central authority, educational reforms were introduced for the purposes of coping with the West and preserving the substance of traditional Chinese culture, but these did not create the necessary social and political conditions. It was like grafting a small branch of the Western tree to the Chinese plant, and hoping for its luxuriant growth without providing the necessary soil and climatic conditions.

Later, during the Republican era, while the modern, Western-oriented intelligentsia began to display greater maturity in espousing new educational programs, the combined impact of internal strife and external aggression rendered educational progress on a broad front virtually impossible. There were isolated cases of outstanding educational accomplishments, but the nation as a whole continued to suffer from the evils of illiteracy, technical incompetence, and an outmoded educational system, which left the masses where they had been for centuries. In terms of education, China's tragic lesson is this: Since educational reform was not an integral part of a larger effort, it failed to contribute to the progress of the nation as a whole, and lack of progress materially aided the rise of Communism. Thus, from Confucian humanism and the selection of an elite, the pendulum of Chinese education has swung to dialectical materialism and the creation of Socialist Man.

In studying Chinese education under Communism, it must be borne in mind that the entire Communist movement is fundamentally an educational task, its success or failure dependent on the degree to which the Chinese population are "educated" to accept and work for the achievement of Communist goals. Under Communism, education forms an integral part of the national plan, leaves no one out of reach, and is directed by a single source of authority. It is, in a word, totalitarian.

Totalitarianism is, indeed, the dominant theme of contemporary Chinese national life. Politically, totalitarianism has meant the elimination of all real and potential forces of opposition and the establishment of a government with absolute power. Through the government machinery and party apparatus, the Communists now control all aspects of national activity. By insisting on party leadership in education, the regime is able to pursue its educational goals with a singleness of purpose and a degree of effectiveness unprecedented in Chinese history. Through the use of modern means of communication, the power of the central government is felt in every corner of the vast country, and the educational programs adopted by the party hierarchy are implemented with all speed and with unquestioning faith by a growing army of militant and disciplined party members. Preferring persuasion to coercion, education has become the chief weapon of political indoctrination, by means of which the state is able to enforce ideological uniformity.

Economically, totalitarianism has meant the concentration of power in the hands of the state through its control of all means of production. The state collects and dispenses, builds and destroys, advances and retreats according to a gigantic economic plan. By eliminating non-state sources of economic power, the Communists have succeeded in reducing every Chinese to small cogs in an enormous economic machine which performs the state-assigned functions of production. Such an economic structure has great implications for education. Education now occupies a prominent position in the formulation of economic plans and represents an important item of economic investment in financial as well as manpower terms. The training of technical personnel—from geologists to find hidden resources to semiskilled workers to operate simple machines—is calculated on the basis of the nation's economic needs. To carry out the principle requiring the combination of education and productive labor direct use is made of a large army of students for economic purposes, and the emphasis on scientism will eventually create a generation of technically qualified workers who will transform China into an industrial power.

Totalitarianism has also meant the introduction of new means of social control. Traditional areas of personal loyalty have been steadily undermined and the value system which sustained the old pattern of human relations has been radically altered. The state, under the direction of the Communist Party, is now the supreme object of allegiance and even of worship. Family solidarity, clan loyalty, love of one's native place, are denounced as feudal traits unworthy of the new Socialist Man, while religion is equated with superstition, and is to be overcome by socialist and scientific education. There can be no voluntary social associations other than the political organizations, labor unions, cooperatives, and the multitude of social organs sponsored or at least tolerated by the Communist Party. Traditional codes of morality have been revised to become socialist morality, the essence of the new Socialist Man. It is, therefore, not possible to exaggerate the importance of education when a nation of China's size and population attempts to create a new social order, new human relations, new values, and a new self-image in accordance with a new ideology.

The totalitarian character of contemporary China is symbolized best, perhaps, by the organization and functions of the communes. As basic units of political control, economic cooperation, and social cohesion, the communes are organs in which substantial numbers of the Chinese people are grouped and their thoughts and action regimented. Following the policy of decentralization, the communes, since 1958, have been given the responsibility of establishing schools of various descriptions, ranging from literacy classes to elementary, middle, and vocational schools, to Red-and-Expert colleges. Commune members receive their political indoctrination through attendance at these schools which are conducted, as a rule, by tested and trusted cadres. Sessions devoted to "thought examination" are held from time to time to inculcate the sense of belonging, to raise the level of "political consciousness," and to convince the skeptical of the correctness of the party line.

In addition to the regular schools on the elementary and junior middle levels, most communes now operate spare-time and vocational schools where the more promising youth receive technical training of one form or another, geared primarily to the particular needs of the commune's economic development. The regime seems fully to realize the necessity of developing education on the grass-roots level, not only because of the inadequacy of government educational facilities but also because of the sociological effect of making education available to the vast majority of the Chinese people who were denied education in the past.

Regardless of the viewpoint of the investigator of contemporary Chinese affairs, the inescapable impression is that one-fifth of mankind is being re-educated and remade with prodigious effort. Aggressive nationalism has replaced traditional humanism, and the major objective of education—now heavily scientific and technical—has become the maximization of national power through industrialization. The present phase of China's march into modernity is one of release of national energy, for which education provides both the direction and the key. Inasmuch as the Chinese leaders themselves are keenly aware of the international implications of China's experiment, sustained study of Chinese education under Communism promises to shed considerable light on China's own development as well as on her place in the family of nations.

## II

The reprinting of this volume provides an opportunity for supplementing the earlier introduction with an examination of what may be called the record of educational performance since the founding of the People's Republic of China. While the "general line" of educational thought and objectives, as discussed in the earlier introduction, has remained largely unchanged, the pattern of educational development during the past twenty-five or so years has been far from uniform. Intricately involved in the waxing and waning of ideological and political forces, the front line of China's educational revolution has shifted considerably over the years. What follows is an attempt to give a general view of the changing educational scene up to the post-Cultural Revolution phase.

### THE NEW SYSTEM OF EDUCATION

At the time of the Communist accession to power, there existed two major types of schools on all levels. On the one hand there were those established by the Communists in areas under their control since the war years. Because of both the backward and destitute conditions then prevailing in these areas and the ideological and political stance of the Communist movement, these schools were without exception of a make-shift nature, having no such institutional provisions as procedures for admission, curriculum, and requirements for graduation. Irrespective of the names by which they were known, the schools found in the so-called "old-liberated areas" were no more than training centers of one sort or another, usually of relatively short duration. In other words, they shared the common characteristic of being informal and unstructured. Also, by virtue of the insurgent character of the Communist movement, the schools were first and foremost designed to serve some specific political purpose, ranging from the training of party cadres to the preparation of theatrical workers in the countryside. It was estimated that, at the time of Communist takeover, about 15 per cent of all schools in China belonged to this category.[1] Constituting the majority of the schools then functioning were those operated or approved by the Nationalist government, which can be divided into government and private schools, of which the latter can be further divided into those in the hands of the Chinese and those financed and controlled by foreign missions.

The Communist regime was dissatisfied with both the Nationalist system which they inherited and with the schools of their own creation for the lack of a system. If the Nationalist educational legacy was found unacceptable for ideological reasons, the earlier Communist educational institutions were considered too unstructured to be used as a basis for the new system. After almost two years of consolidating and adjusting, the then Government Administration Council announced on October 1, 1951 its resolutions concerning the reform of China's educational system. Enumerating the shortcomings of the current system of education, this document mentioned the following: 1. there are no recognized positions in the system for the various types of informal schools for the peasants and workers; 2. the difficulties encountered by the masses in receiving complete primary education; and 3. the absence of systematic organization for technical education.[2]

Anticipating further difficulties in the future, the resolutions nevertheless laid down guidelines for the steady development of education in China, within the institutional framework which the resolutions provided.

Considering the regime's rejection of the old and ambition for the new, the new system of education of 1951 cannot but be regarded as a mild piece of reform.

1 Editorial, *Jen-min chiao-yu,* vol. 1, no. 3, July 1, 1951, p. 9.
2 *Jen-min jih-pao,* October 1, 1951.

Indeed, the graphic presentation of the new system drew rather wide-spread skeptical response as to its revolutionary character.[3] At the same time, an editorial in the *People's Daily* declared, "any system of education is the reflection of a society's productive and scientific conditions; the level of productive and scientific conditions attained by or potentially attainable to a society dictates that society's system of education." Inasmuch' as the regime was at that time beset by enormous problems arising from the need to consolidate its power within and to conduct a war in Korea, it is perhaps understandable that efforts were made to avoid extraordinarily radical approaches to reforming education. Be that as it may, the new system was indicative of some of the fundamental principles of education advocated by the Communists. It sought, in the first place, to change the social meaning of education by "opening the doors of schools to peasants and workers." By shortening the primary phase of education to five years and doing away with the division into junior (four years) and senior (two years) grades, the new system aimed at the gradual universalization of primary education. (It was made clear at the time of announcement that the new system of primary education was to take effect beginning in 1952 and to be completed in five years.) Secondly, the new system provided, on all levels, what may be described as supplementary schools of various types which run parallel to the regular schools. Whereas this was to a certain extent also true of the pre-Communist days, the true significance of the new system lies in its provision of transferability; that is, students are now enabled to cross the institutional bridge between the formal and less formal tracks. Thirdly, in keeping with the spirit of promoting universal education, at no level of education is there any limitation of age, so that unlettered and uneducated adults and adolescents are encouraged to receive primary education in either accelerated or spare-

[3] Answers to questions concerning the new system of education, *People's Education*, vol. 4, no. 1, November 1951, p. 36.

time primary schools. The same is true of secondary and higher education. Lastly, there was a clear emphasis upon the practicality of education, in keeping with the pronounced objective of adapting education to the economic, political, and defense needs of the nation, especially in the area of economic development.[4]

During the period 1950–1953, while primary and secondary education underwent considerable consolidation and expansion, major changes took place on the higher education level. Partly because of the social and cultural significance of higher education, but more importantly because of the pressing needs for high-level trained personnel at a time of all-out national reconstruction, the regime found it necessary to revamp higher education in accordance with specific ideological, economic, and pedagogical principles. For the purposes of understanding the objective conditions and problems in higher education, determining the objectives and functions of higher education, reorganizing the administrative structure and curriculum, and exchanging views concerning leadership, rearrangement of colleges and departments, and the despatch of students abroad, the first National Conference on Higher Education was held in Peking in July 1950.[5] Out of this conference came some of the most fundamental decisions, particularly in respect to the matters of leadership and curriculum reform.[6] Organizationally, this period witnessed the most sweeping changes in higher education, through merging, reorganization, and creation of new institutions.

By the end of 1953, as a result of a series of readjustments, the number of institutions of higher learning had been reduced from two hundred twenty-seven to one hun-

---

[4] Ma Hsu-lun, Opening speech at the first national higher education conference, *People's Education*, vol. 1, no. 3, July 1, 1950, p. 12.

[5] *People's Education*, vol. 1, no. 1, May 1950, p. 16.

[6] For English translation of these decisions, see Stewart Fraser, *Chinese Communist Education* (Nashville, Tenn.: Vanderbilt University Press, 1965), pp. 92–97.

dred eighty-two. The reorganization plan was implemented on the basis of some overriding considerations: 1. more efficient and economical utilization of available resources, both material and human; 2. greater emphasis on scientific and technological education; 3. elimination of foreign-supported institutions; and 4. strengthening of educational leadership both for planning and for administration. Geographically, the two regions of North China and East China were taken as points of emphasis, with Peking and Tientsin as focal points for North China and Shanghai and Nanking for East China. After reorganization, North China had a total of forty-one universities and colleges and East China had fifty-four. In both regions, all foreign missionary institutions were abolished.[7] The new pattern of higher education that emerged out of the long process of reorganization showed three major types of institutions of higher learning. The first consisted of fourteen comprehensive universities, spread over all parts of the country, which included several colleges with a number of academic disciplines represented; the second group was made up of multi-subject polytechnical institutes, emphasizing science and technology and usually bearing the name "university," such as Tsing-hua University in Peking and Chekiang University in Hangchow. The third group, numerically the largest, was composed of single-subject institutes, ranging from medicine, to petroleum, to teacher training and language training.[8]

In curriculum and teaching reform, the early 1950's

[7] In the North, the Catholic Fu-jen University and the Protestant Yen-ching University, both in Peking, were abolished; in East China, Ching-ling in Nanking, Ch'i-lu in Chinan, St. John's, Shanghai, and Aurora in Shanghai ceased to exist. *People's Daily*, Peking, September 24, 1952.

[8] At the end of 1953, there existed in Mainland China 14 comprehensive universities, 39 technical universities and colleges, 31 normal colleges, 29 agricultural and forestry colleges, 29 medical colleges, 4 political and legal institutes, 6 economic and financial institutes, 8 language institutes, 15 Fine Arts schools, 5 physical education colleges, and 2 national minority institutes. *People's Daily*, December 17, 1953.

saw the steady growth of Soviet influence, China in those days being declared "leaning to one side." Increasingly large numbers of Soviet pedagogists and educational specialists came to China to take part in the planning, improvement, and reform in all aspects of the educational task, and it is estimated that more than seven thousand such Soviet experts were working in China at the end of 1957. They were credited with rendering valuable assistance to the designing of new courses and the compilation of new texts.[9]

Viewed against the general background of revolutionary turmoil in the early 1950's when such nation-wide campaigns as Resist-America Aid-Korea, Land Reform, the Three-Anti and Five-Anti campaigns gripped the minds of the entire population, the educational front appears to have been relatively calm. Nevertheless, inasmuch as the new system of education had grown out of some of the fundamental ideological considerations, without due regard for the actual socio-economic conditions then prevailing, implementation of the new system ran into difficulties within a short period of time. For example, the new five-year primary school, designed for the purpose of universalizing primary education by shortening the period from six to five years, failed to achieve its goal and reverted to the former four-year, two-year system at the end of 1953. The Communist authorities obviously overestimated both the speed and degree of economic recovery, especially in the rural areas; the reduction of one year meant actually the addition of another year to the earlier four-year lower primary phase, at a time when the majority of rural children were needed for farming work at home. The inability of rural families to spare their children for five years of schooling and the serious shortage of both

[9] It was reported that the Soviet experts helped with the introduction of and improvement upon 889 curriculum courses, edited and compiled 629 textbooks, and translated and published 1,393 titles of college and university texts. Fang Cheng, "Communist China's Educational Revolution," *The China Monthly*, no. 45, December 1967, p. 3.

teachers and teaching materials combined to render in-
effectual the new system on the primary level. Likewise,
the accelerated middle schools for peasants and workers,
while defensible as an auxiliary educational arrangement, proved to be entirely unworkable as an integral
part of the educational system. The exceedingly low
quality of education provided in these schools prevented most of the graduates from entering into higher
institutions while those who did enter presented serious
problems to the institutions to which they had been
admitted. Finally, these accelerated middle schools were
ordered to suspend admission in 1955.[10]

In spite of the difficulties encountered and the adjust-
ments made, the first five years of Communist rule saw
a considerable increase in the number of both schools
and students. The percentage increases in 1953-54 over
the pre-1949 peak were as follows:

| | |
|---|---|
| Higher institutions | 140% |
| Secondary schools | 193% |
| Primary schools | 218% |
| Kindergartens | 326% |

With the advent of the first Five-Year Plan in 1953,
China's system of education began to stabilize under the
two cardinal principles of "education must be in the
service of proletarian politics" and "education must be
combined with productive labor." Following Mao Tse-
tung's dictum that "with the arrival of the high tide of
Socialist economic development, there will inevitably
be a cultural high tide," [11] the educational front witnessed considerable and consistent expansion. Three
developments were particularly significant during the
period of the first Five-Year Plan and they deserve closer
attention.

In keeping with the overriding concern with proletarian politics, emphasis in education understandably

[10] *New China Monthly,* Peking, July 1955, p. 227.
[11] Quoted in *Ten Great Years* (Peking: State Statistics Bureau, People's Publishing House, 1959), p. 166.

## THE GREAT LEAP FORWARD IN EDUCATION AND ITS AFTERMATH

Despite the shortcomings and problems which became manifest during the initial phase of consolidation and later the period of expansion, the education scene, like other facets of Chinese national life under Communism up to 1957, displayed, on the whole, signs of stability and growth. If, as many charged, popularization had meant the lowering of academic standards, emphasis on politics the stifling of free thought, and borrowing from Soviet experience merely slavish imitation of educational practices of dubious value, the development of education during the period up to 1957 nevertheless had been quite substantial when viewed against the perspective of the immediate past and of the ideological strictures of Communism. However, with the launching of the Great Leap Forward Campaign in 1958, accompanied by the commune movement, the entire country was plunged into a state of frenzy. Total mobilization of the population for the fullest utilization of material resources was the declared policy, aimed at the development of China on all fronts in the shortest period of time. In education, the Great Leap meant expansion on all levels at a breakneck speed, under the general slogans, "education must be in the service of proletarian politics" and "education must be combined with productive labor."

In November 1958, in the wake of the Great Leap, an exhibition was held in the capital city of Peking to show, with charts, graphs, and other visual devices, the impressive gains and triumphs that had been achieved through the combination of education with productive labor. In a congratulatory editorial marking the opening of the exhibition, the *People's Daily* reaffirmed the correctness of the Party line in stressing the principles of education. Among other claims, the numbers of schools and students enrolled on all levels were reported to have increased by leaps and bounds, as indicated in the following table.[19]

| | Number of Schools | Number of Students | Percentage Increase Schools | Percentage Increase Students |
|---|---|---|---|---|
| Higher Education | 1,408 | 790,000 | 515 | 80 |
| Secondary Education | 118,000 | 15,000,000 | 846 | 112 |
| Primary Education | 950,000 | 92,000,000 | 73 | 43 |

Other equally impressive "leaps" were reported to have been registered on all fronts. Citing concrete examples, the *Education Semi-Monthly* reported that the Department of Economics of Nankai University, working collectively and abiding by the principle of combining academic work with production, completed, within forty days, various research projects totaling four million words, while prior to that, over a much longer period of time, fewer than a million words of written work had been completed.[20] While academic research represented one part of the process of education, productive activities were equally stressed. It was therefore reported that, in the field of steel-making, some 21,000 schools erected 14,400 steel furnaces which were expected to produce 1,590,000 tons of steel by the end of 1958.

Abiding by the oft-repeated slogan of "To, K'uai, Hao, Sheng," meaning "more (in quantity), faster (in time), better (in quality), cheaper (in expenditure)," all those involved in education sought to soar to new heights on the statistical chart, with the result that many claims tended to defy credulity. Moreover, since the quality of education by any standard was difficult, if not impossible, to visually or statistically measure, no attempt was made to evaluate educational progress in qualitative terms. By the end of 1959, it became obvious that the

19 Editorial, *People's Daily*, November 1, 1958.
20 *Education Semi-Monthly*, no. 21, 1958, p. 12.

Leap in education, though impressive in quantitative terms, had not only exacted a heavy price in quality but also given rise to serious problems. Since productive labor formed the cornerstone of the educational Leap, teachers and students in regular full-time schools were required to participate in productive labor for an average period of three months each year, exclusive of special "crash" projects which were numerous. For part-time and spare-time schools of various types, the amount of time devoted to labor was proportionally higher.

A major change of this nature in educational practices, involving millions of students and educational workers, would require an enormous amount of planning and coordination to insure that education did not suffer because of the reduction of class and study time, and that labor thus expended would prove productive. Inasmuch as the entire Leap campaign was primarily based upon a highly exaggerated estimate of both material and human resources, and an unrealistic belief in the ability of the Party's propaganda machine to generate popular enthusiasm, the campaign proved disastrous on all essential fronts. In the field of education, failure of the Great Leap provoked harsh criticisms, understandably more out-spoken among students, their parents, and certain segments of the teaching profession.

A review of mainland Chinese publications in the latter part of 1959 indicated that there was wide-spread dissatisfaction with the policy then in force. Some of the most persistent criticisms stemmed from a fundamental doubt about the wisdom of emphasizing productive labor to the extent that was done at that time. The critical view which gained considerable currency was that what was lost by the Leap far outweighed the gains. According to this view, the entire program resulted in the "waste of golden youth." In specific terms, the critics charged that the practice of sending students to the rural areas deprived them of the opportunity to pursue their educational goals under trained teachers, while pitifully little was learned from the examples afforded of "model workers." After admitting that certain beneficial results had been derived from productive labor in terms of physical development and socialist morality, they insisted that intellectual growth had suffered greatly, a situation succinctly summed up in the phrase "two high and one low."

More importantly, the so-called merging of schools with factories and farms created a situation so chaotic that the normal educational process was seriously disrupted. Teachers were unable to follow their teaching plans while students were at a loss to know what course of action to pursue. Students suffered from confusion in identity; they were both students and workers, yet they were neither students nor workers. Under such circumstances, more and more students withdrew from schools, some of their own volition because of a loss of faith in the educational future, others at the behest of their parents. The popular view prevailed that, since the Party seemed determined to transform students into workers who, although without formal education, were comparatively well treated, there was no longer much point in trying to seek education as a path to personal advancement.

It must be borne in mind that the Leap in education formed part of a much larger movement which sought to propel China helter-skelter into the modern industrial age. Consequently, the emphasis upon productive labor can be readily appreciated in pure economic terms—to utilize a reserve of available able-bodied manpower. More important, however, was the political objective of bringing up a new generation of socialist men, dedicated to the task of building socialism according to the tenets of Marxism–Leninism–Maoism. Participation in labor was therefore considered an effective means of developing in the students a proletarian outlook and a proper respect for labor, at the same time preventing them from becoming isolated from the masses. The concern with political correctness necessitated, among other things, a firm control over education by the Communist Party, whose educational cadres emphasized redness at the expense of expertness, resulting in a general lowering of academic standards on all levels. Further opportunities for education, as well as future careers. became dependent upon the assessment of political reliability of individual students by the Party functionaries. There developed, as the Leap gathered momentum, a widespread skepticism about the need and even the wisdom of acquiring substantive knowledge, a process which was rendered increasingly difficult by the disruptive effects of productive labor. As a consequence, in addition to specific charges against the excesses in stressing labor, there was criticism of the extent to which political considerations were allowed to interfere with the educational process.

## THE PERIOD OF RETRENCHMENT

In the wake of the Great Leap and its attendant dislocation, the regime found it necessary to bring about still another set of changes. Without abandoning slogans, the regime, beginning in 1960, introduced a series of corrective measures which resulted in a tactical shift on the educational front. Of first importance was the shift in emphasis from redness to expertness, although the slogan "Red and Expert" remained as the ultimate of educational aims. From 1960 on, publications on the mainland began to stress the importance of academic excellence and to exhort the students to greater scholarly efforts. On the occasion of a graduation exercise in 1961, Vice Premier Chen Yi, speaking for the Party, cautioned against undue emphasis on politics in education. He went so far as to state that, since the socialist reconstruction of China required the service of unnumbered specialists of all descriptions, each student must endeavor to demonstrate his political consciousness through the acquisition and application of special knowledge and skills, sophistication in politics in the narrow sense being a matter of secondary importance.[21]

With the political line more or less redrawn and clari-

[21] *Kuang-ming Daily,* September 3, 1961.

fied, there was also a notable change in the labor aspect of education. A considerably more rational approach was adopted, and students worked in factories or on farms more for economic gain than for purely political training. Moreover, the duration and the timing of the period of labor were regulated in such a way as to minimize disruption of school work, while due consideration was given to the specialties of students in the assignment of type of labor to be performed.

Organizationally, the frenzied attempt to expand at all cost was abandoned in favor of consolidation. Such practices as elevating secondary technical school to the rank of higher institutions, splitting one school into two, and arbitrary reshuffling of teaching personnel, all of which contributed to the chaos of the Leap, were discontinued. At the same time, schools that existed no more than in name and were clearly of inferior quality were either abolished or merged with others. Claims of great quantitative expansion became less frequent and, when made, tended to be more reserved in tone. Since the Party's control over education was completely assured, there was also the tendency toward granting a larger degree of autonomy in educational matters to regional and local authorities, as well as encouraging such productive organizations as communes and industrial plants to establish and maintain their own educational facilities. The fundamental objective of expanding at a fast pace but minimal cost still remained, but greater attention seemed to be paid to the qualitative aspect of education in the early 1960's than during the initial stages of the Leap.

The consolidation and retrenchment program had some notable features which were indicative of some new trends at that time. On the pre-school and primary level, major emphasis continued to be on the universalization of primary education, which had achieved impressive results by the end of 1958. After 1962, efforts were made in the direction of expanding primary boarding schools and raising the quality of teachers as well as the quality of primary education itself. In higher education, the pace of expansion slowed down and a reexamination of the existing institutions took place with a view to meeting more effectively the demand for technically competent personnel. Most of the "red and expert" colleges and universities which mushroomed during the Leap were either discontinued or reorganized.

It was, however, on the secondary level that the most significant changes were introduced. In some respects, secondary education during the Leap had proved to be a weak link between the primary phase below and the higher phase above. Regular full-time secondary schools had found it difficult to meet the needs of primary school graduates and at the same time had failed to provide higher institutions with qualified candidates in sufficient numbers. Because of this deficiency, the agricultural middle school movement found great impetus as a remedial device.

The agricultural middle schools admitted students of the thirteen-to-sixteen age group and operated on a half-day basis. Their curriculum was identical with that of the junior middle schools, but in addition to regular subjects, the students were required to learn through active work on farms those technical skills which would qualify them to serve as agricultural technicians. Inasmuch as there were some thirty-seven million Chinese in the thirteen-to-seventeen age group, and only a little over seven million were enrolled in full-time secondary schools, the agricultural middle schools, numbering some thirty thousand and with three million students in 1960, became a very important part of the educational scene.

Taken together, the retrenchment period witnessed a reversal of the earlier position of ideological rigidity that characterized the Great Leap. More specifically, the retrenchment meant the re-establishment of normal teaching processes, noninterference with academic work by Party cadres, the shortening of periods for productive labor, encouragement of scientific experiment, proper respect for scholars, and the steady improvement of education in general. The swinging of the pendulum in the direction of normalcy and rationality was accompanied by a general relaxation in the government's policy in the fields of art, literature, and cultural affairs. As a result of this policy shift, conditions in education and other fields improved markedly, and a feeling of "contentment and satisfaction" generally prevailed on most campuses. During this period of relative stability, conditions in general in China were also improving, as can be seen in the overall improvement in agriculture, the expansion of foreign trade, industrial growth, and in science and technology a successful series of nuclear explosions.

It was also during this period of retrenchment that the principle of "two kinds of educational systems" was adopted and implemented. Announced in August, 1964, the new principle had the sponsorship on no less a personage than Liu Shao-chi, and meant simply the maintenance of the *status quo* in regard to full-time schools, on the one hand, and all-out expansion of half-work half-study schools, on the other. For the purpose of promoting the latter type of education, administratively there were now additional government organs, usually known as the Second Education Bureau (or Commission or Section, depending on the level of administration), charged with implementing policies regarding half-work half-study education. Moreover, for the purpose of formulating the most effective and practicable policies, a series of conferences both on the national and regional levels was held in different parts of the country.[22]

Given the general conditions then prevailing, and in view of the discrepancy between educational demand and educational resources, the policy of "two kinds of educational systems" was not without merit, especially when it is considered that the policy called for "five years of experimentation and ten years of steady expan-

[22] From March 1965 to the end of the same year five national conferences were held, under the sponsorship of the Ministry of Education, Ministry of Higher Education, Ministry of Health, and Ministry of Agriculture. By the end of August 1965, nineteen provinces and autonomous regions had held regional conferences to discuss the various problems involved in the development of half-work half-study education. See *China Monthly*, no. 45, December 1967, p. 4.

sion." Indeed, the stabilization of the educational scene during this whole period was at least partly attributable to this policy.

## THE GREAT PROLETARIAN CULTURAL REVOLUTION AND ITS IMPACT ON EDUCATION

In both scope and intensity, the Cultural Revolution which began in the spring of 1966 undoubtedly represented the most sweeping and far-reaching phase of change in the entire history of China under Communism. The Revolution indicated still another swing to the left of the pendulum of Chinese national life. Largely as a result of the emergence of a new pattern during the period of retrenchment, to the zealous revolutionaries led by and identified with Mao himself, China in 1966 was showing every sign of abandoning the true objectives of revolution and compromising on the ideological front. Those in power, under the leadership of Liu Shao-chi, were accused of "taking the capitalist road" and of leading China down the path of revisionism. The overriding purpose of the Cultural Revolution, therefore, was the seizure of power from the "revisionists" so as to create a new society in accordance with the blueprint of Mao.

To education, the Cultural Revolution meant not only the reversal of the revisionist trend but more importantly the mobilization of students as active agents of the Revolution, enabling them to wage revolutionary struggles on their own and to acquire experiences which would insure ideological correctness in the future. Known as the Red Guard, the student revolutionaries vigorously attacked what they contemptuously called revisionist education and demanded faithful adherence to the Maoist formula of socialist education.[23]

[23] For a Red Guard version of the long struggle between the two schools of thought concerning education, see "Chronology of the Two-Road Struggle on the Education Front in the Past Seventeen Years," in *Chiao-yu ko-ming* (*Educational Revolution*), May 6, 1967. (English translation in *Chinese Education—A Journal of Translations*, vol. 1, no. 1, Spring 1968.)

In the context of the Cultural Revolution, the first significant statement by Mao concerning education was made on May 7, 1966, in a letter to Lin Piao, his newly designated heir-apparent, in which he directed that "the students' major concern is academic study, but they must study other subjects. This means they have to study not only liberal arts, but also engineering, agricultural and military sciences, as well as criticize the bourgeoisie. The curriculum must be shortened and there must be an educational revolution. The phenomenon in which our schools are dominated by bourgeois intellectuals cannot be allowed to continue." [24] Inspired by what has since become known as the "May 7 instruction" of Mao, several students at Peking University, led by a junior member of the faculty, put up one of the first "big-character posters" on May 25, 1966, in which they accused the president and other administrators of the University of following capitalist principles and practices of education, thereby attempting to create a new generation of bourgeois intellectuals and to negate the achievements of socialist education. A few days later, Mao personally endorsed the revolutionary position of the students by ordering that the contents of the big-character poster be broadcast over Radio Peking. From then on, the educational part of the Cultural Revolution spread to all parts of the country, resulting in a complete reexamination of the educational record of China and the pouring forth of a variety of recommendations and demands for the restructure of Chinese education.

It scarcely needs mention that the educational part of the Cultural Revolution was only one aspect of the larger struggle, coinciding with the reassertion of power by Mao and his supporters and the removal from positions of power of Liu Shao-chi and those identified with his so-called revisionist policy lines. In concrete terms, the educational revolution began with the dismissal of some of the top-ranking administrators in leading institutions, including such universities as Peking, Wuhan,

24 *Ibid.,* p. 57.

and Nanking.[25] Without exception, these leading per-
sonalities were accused of reintroducing capitalism into
Chinese education, going against the teachings of Chairman Mao, closing the doors of schools to members of
the proletariat, encouraging intellectualism with its
social aloofness, and, in general, following the road of
revisionism. Once the responsible individuals were removed from positions of power, there followed a period
in which the revolutionaries gave vent to their griev-
ances and criticized all aspects of education at that time.
Broadly, the Maoist revolutionaries were intensely dissatisfied with the fundamentally "traditional and capitalist" approach to education, which manifested itself in
several essential ways. First, the system by which educational opportunities were distributed was considered an
unmistakable vestige of the discredited past in that the
major means of selection continued to be competitive
examination, reminiscent of the centuries-old imperial
examination system. Continuation of this system meant
therefore not only the rejection of promising students
of proletarian origin who formed the majority, but also
the creation of an academic minority or elite. Secondly,
emphasis upon academic performance, a natural by-
product of the examination system, had given rise to a
situation in which the students were primarily concerned
with academic excellence at the expense of politics.
Thirdly, the revisionist educational policy had defeated
the very purposes of socialist education by weakening
the students intellectually through force-feeding, morally
through encouraging individualism, and physically
through meaningless overwork.

The overthrow of power-holders was followed by a
period of intense power seizure which was by no means
confined to educational power. In the field of education,
however, the downfall of what may be called the Establishment headed by Liu led to a torrent of public criti-

[25] For a study of the impact of the Cultural Revolution on
higher education, see C. T. Hu, "The Chinese University:
Target of the Cultural Revolution," *Saturday Review*, August
19, 1967.

cism from all levels of education and all parts of the country. Whether general or specific, concerning theory or practice, all criticisms had the common objective of destroying the established order and the common ideological framework of Maoism. In the wake of such criticisms, a series of changes were introduced, some with the authority of the state, and others by the new revolutionary committees which had taken over the administration of the majority of the schools.

Like other facets of Chinese life, education of the young remains in a state of flux, although nearly a decade has elapsed since the launching of the Great Cultural Revolution. Insofar as the changes are concerned, abandonment of earlier beliefs and practices has been more prominent than adoption of new measures. As a direct response to the demands of revolutionary students, the Central Committee of the Chinese Communist Party and the State Council jointly announced the suspension of entrance examinations for all higher institutions on June 15, 1966.[26] This act had the effect of releasing a considerable number of students for revolutionary activities, by and large through Red Guard organizations. The revolutionary activities of the Red Guards officially began on August 18, when Mao received personally the "revolutionary teachers and students" at Tien-an-men in Peking. From that day on, the students no longer concerned themselves with purely educational affairs but plunged into the all-encompassing task of "making revolution" on a nation-wide basis. Inspired by some of the earlier exploits of the Chinese Communist Party, the students gave their organizations various names to commemorate such events as the uprising in Chingkangshan and the Long March. In December 1966, fifteen students, representing the Maritime College in Dairen, walked from their school to Peking, over a distance of two thousand *li*, under the banner of "Long March Red Guard Detachment." [27] Hundreds of Red Guard units appeared from all parts of the coun-

[26] *People's Daily,* Peking, June 18, 1966.
[27] *People's Daily,* Peking, December 22, 1966.

try, dedicated to power seizure, routing the rightists and revisionists, and exchanging revolutionary experiences among themselves by traveling all over the country. They completely destroyed the educational system then in use, and in so doing plunged the whole nation into the abyss of chaos.

In February and March 1967, the Central Committee of the Chinese Communist Party issued, in quick succession, three directives ordering all students to return to their schools and to resume their revolutionary activities on campus.[28] These directives exhorted the students to continue the cultural revolution in their own schools, to form alliances with the masses, to study Mao's works diligently, and above all, to work out a plan for education in the future that would conform to the intent and spirit of the Cultural Revolution. Return to the schools, however, did not mean resumption of the educational process. Indeed, with the institutional framework irreparably smashed and the last vestige of authority destroyed, it was physically impossible for a normal educational process to go on. In the few schools where a semblance of normalcy prevailed, instruction has been confined to the works of Mao.

Inasmuch as the Great Cultural Revolution still grips the nation, the educational scene remains exceedingly confusing and unstable. However, as long as the objectives of the Revolution are sought, there can be little doubt that the system of the pre-Revolution days has been abandoned. Although the Communist Party and the state have not officially adopted a new system to replace the old, there is sufficient evidence to show that the new type of education in China will have some highly revolutionary features.

With respect to admission, the system of recommendation and selection will be employed. For primary schools, the entering age will be reduced from seven to

[28] The directive for primary schools was issued on February 18, those for secondary and higher institutions on March 3 and 11 respectively. See *Wen-hui Daily,* Shanghai, of those dates.

## CHINESE EDUCATION IN THE NINETEEN SEVENTIES*

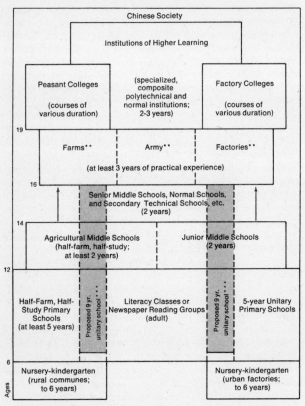

*Adapted from the tentative schema developed by Stewart E. Fraser in collaboration with
John N. Hawkins and S. C. Hu.
**Schools run by farms, military or political organs, and factories are not shown.
***A nationwide unitary school of nine years has been proposed for ages 7-15.

six, while higher institutions will no longer impose age limitations on students, nor will married students be excluded. The most significant development, however, has to do with the distribution of educational opportunities. To prevent the bourgeoisie from reasserting itself, priorities for admissions into all schools will be given students of peasant, worker, and soldier origins. Recognizing the influential role of teachers, this admission policy calling for preferential treatment for the proletariat will be adhered to with special vigor in the case of normal schools. Scholarships and subsidies likewise will be increased for the benefit of members of the proletariat.

One of the most persistent criticisms against the old system of education has been the alienation of students from the masses. This, to the revolutionary elements, is attributable primarily to the long duration of schooling which tends to foster the feeling of aloofness and the spirit of elitism among students. Shortening the period of schooling is considered imperative; the current demand is that both the primary and secondary phases be reduced from six to four or five years, and that higher education should last no longer than four years, with most specialized study reduced to two years. Since the teaching material now in use is the product of the old system, there is demand that new textbooks, outlines, teaching plans, and similar materials be totally revised, using the works of Mao Tse-tung as the fountain of all knowledge.

Pedagogically, the role of teachers appears to be confined to that of preceptor, major emphasis being placed upon the initiative of the students. Under such an arrangement, the system of examination is discontinued, together with the five-grade marking practice borrowed earlier from the Soviet Union. Evaluation of individual students' work will be collectively done by the teacher, the students as a group, and the political cadres of the school, who together form what is referred to as the "educational alliance." In the same spirit, qualifications for advancement into higher institutions and graduation no longer have much to do with academic performance;

instead, they are determined by the Party on the basis of evaluation by the alliance of workers, peasants, and soldiers. Such evaluation, in turn, is based upon the individual students' performance during their participation in the three great revolutionary movements of class struggle, production struggle, and scientific experimentation. Theses and graduation projects are not required of students graduating from institutions of higher learning; in fact, those considered by the educational alliance as superior in their work in the three revolutionary movements are permitted to graduate earlier than others. To qualify for selection for post-graduate work or study abroad, students must have had three to five years of experience in productive labor, acceptable social background, and, above all, ideological rectitude, thoroughly imbued with the thought of Mao Tse-tung.

Political and administrative organs have been established in all schools in strict accordance with the principle of party supremacy and the Maoist concept of democratic centralism. Absolute control over all aspects of school life is insured by entrusting power to the school Party committee, with the administration, faculty, and students forming the alliance for the fulfillment of educational objectives. Both teachers and students are now organized in para-military units, to emulate, in part, the Anti-Japanese College of the war years. Moreover, to wipe out all vestiges of the earlier educational beliefs and practices that have betrayed the Revolution, such symbols as school badges, experimental schools, ranks, and titles have been abolished.[29]

Not until the latter half of 1969 did the schools begin to resume some of their normal functions. By 1974 a new pattern of education has clearly emerged, although regional differences as well as those between levels do exist. The present phase seems to have the characteristics of stressing political education or ideological conditioning,

[29] The plan described above was adopted by the Central Committee of the CCP early in 1967. Details were given in a variety of sources, including reports from Japanese correspondents and journals in Hong Kong.

shortening the period of schooling and simplifying the curriculum, providing preferential treatment in admission and all other aspects for students of worker–peasant–soldier background, combining formal instruction with productive labor, decentralizing administration, and demonstrating a heightened interest in experimenting with new pedagogical ideas and practices.[30]

The creation of the New Socialist Man calls for a complete remaking of the Chinese, in thought, behavior, attitudes, values, and aspirations. Mao and his followers are painfully aware of the magnitude and difficulty of the task which requires, above all else, a cultural and social revolution of a continuing nature. The current anti-Confucius and anti-Lin Piao campaign is, in this sense, no more than a fresh effort at keeping the revolutionary spirit alive, so that the necessary political and cultural climate can be maintained for the educational revolution to go on.

On the educational front, experiments of many kinds are being carried out in various parts of the country and at all levels of the educational ladder, but a new national pattern has yet to emerge. There are, to use Mao's language, many contradictions in the current educational scene, such as those between redness and expertness, political conformity and intellectual creativity, general education and special training, central and regional control, to mention only a few. Again, to use Mao's dictum, there can be no construction without destruction, nor can there be progress without contradictions in the dialectical sense. By any standard, the educational revolution in China under Communism can be said to represent the most sweeping, profound, and ambitious form of human and social engineering ever attempted, and as such it promises to have great impact not only upon China as a nation but also upon the rest of the world.

[30] For an up-to-date analysis of post-Cultural Revolution developments, see Robert D. Barendsen, *The Educational Revolution in China* (Washington, D.C.: U.S. Government Printing Office, 1973).

## BIBLIOGRAPHICAL NOTES

Works on traditional Chinese education in Western languages are rather limited in number and in scope. Of lasting interest is the study by H. S. Galt, *The Development of Chinese Educational Theory* (Shanghai, 1929). Another work of monographic nature is *A Study in Chinese Principles of Education* by Chiang Monlin, one of the most eminent educators in modern China (Shanghai, 1924). Since most of the thinkers in traditional China developed their educational philosophies within the context of Confucian thought, even a cursory perusal of the Confucian classics will go a long way in providing some insight into the philosophical framework of traditional Chinese education. Although there are thirteen works which together make up the "classics," the Four Books of *Analects, Mencius, The Great Learning,* and *The Doctrine of the Mean* form the core of educational materials. An excellent translation of the Four Books can be found in James Legge's monumental work, *The Chinese Classics.* For a cogent discussion of Confucian philosophy, see pertinent parts in Fung Yu-lan, *A Short History of Chinese Philosophy,* translated by Derk Bodde (New York, 1948); Liu Wu-chi, *Confucius, His Life and Time* (New York, 1955); and H. G. Creel, *Confucius, the Man and the Myth* (New York, 1949). On the traditional system of education and the early attempts at educational reforms, see Kuo Pin-wen, *The Chinese System of Public Education* (New York, 1915). An earlier work by a French Sinologist, Eduard C. Biot, was published in Paris in 1847, entitled *Essai sur l'histoire de l'instruction publique en Chine.*

The sociological and legal meaning of traditional Chinese education and the examination system has been studied from different points of view and in varying degrees of depth. Of particular interest are Max Weber, "The Chinese Literati," in *From Max Weber: Essays in Sociology* (New York, 1946); and Chung-li Chang, *The Chinese Gentry* (Seattle, Washington, 1955). The status of

Chinese gentry, as distinguished from the scholar-officials, is discussed and analyzed by Fei Hsiao-t'ung in his *China's Gentry* (Chicago, 1953). A historical study of the impact of the Chinese examination system on the West is found in Ssu-yu Teng, "Chinese Influence on the Western Examination System" (*Harvard Journal of Asiatic Studies,* vol. VII, 1943).

The earlier phase of China's attempts at modernization has been studied by a number of Chinese and Western scholars. Leading works include Teng Ssu-yu and John K. Fairbank, *China's Response to the West* (Cambridge, Massachusetts, 1954); Mary C. Wright, *The Last Stand of Chinese Conservatism* (Stanford, California, 1957); Merebeth E. Cameron, *The Reform Movement in China, 1898–1912* (Stanford, California, 1931); and Ernest R. Hughes, *The Invasion of China by the Western World* (London, 1937). The earliest modern schools in China are discussed by Knight Biggerstaff in *The Modern Government Schools in China* (Ithaca, 1961). Broader in scope and dealing with the introduction of the Western system of education in China is *The History of Modern Education in China* by Theodore F. Hsiao (Shanghai, 1935). A brief survey of the development of modern Chinese education is found in the chapter on "Modern Education" by Francis L. H. Pott, in H. F. MacNair, ed., *China* (Berkeley, California, 1946).

For the Republican period, general works include Chu Yu-kuang, *Some Problems of a National System of Education in China: A Study in the Light of Comparative Education* (Shanghai, 1933); Djung Lu-Dzai, *A History of Democratic Education in Modern China* (Shanghai, 1934); Paul Monroe, *A Report on Education in China* (New York, 1922), and *China, A Nation in Evolution* (New York, 1927); and W. T. Tao and C. P. Chen, *Education in China* (Peiping, 1925). Special studies on various aspects of Chinese education are Chang Pe-chin, *The Administrative Reorganization of the Educational System of a County in China Based on the Analysis of Cheng Ting Hsien* (Ithaca, 1935); Chang Peng-chun, *Education for Modernization in China: A Search for*

*Criteria of Curriculum Construction in View of the Transition in National Life, with Special Reference to Secondary Education* (New York, 1923); Cyrus H. Peake, *Nationalism and Education in Modern China* (New York, 1932); Victor W. W. S. Purcell, *Problems of Chinese Education* (London, 1936); Louis C. Walmsley, *Western Influence on Chinese Education* (unpublished doctoral thesis, University of Toronto, 1945); Wang Fang-kang, *Japanese Influence on Educational Reforms in China* (Peiping, 1933); and G. R. Twiss, *Science and Education in China* (Shanghai, 1925).

On mass education, two works are of great importance: James Y. C. Yen, *The Mass Education Movement in China* (Shanghai, 1925), and Pearl S. Buck, *Tell the People—Mass Education in China* (New York, 1945).

The political role of Chinese students in the Republican period has been intensely studied. Of special interest are Chow Tse-tsung, *The May Fourth Movement: Intellectual Revolution in Modern China* (Cambridge, Massachusetts, 1960); Kiang Wen-han, *The Ideological Background of the Chinese Student Movement* (New York, 1948); John Dewey, "The Student Revolt in China" (*New Republic,* vol. 20, 1919), and "The Sequel of the Student Revolt" (*New Republic,* February 1920); and Paul Monroe, "Student Politics in China" (*Forum,* vol. 76, 1926).

The moving story of the migration of Chinese colleges and students from the coastal regions to the interior after the outbreak of the Sino-Japanese War in 1937 is told in Hubert Freyn's *Chinese Education in the War* (Shanghai, 1940), and the postwar educational problem is discussed by Alice H. Gregg in *China and Educational Autonomy* (Syracuse, 1946).

The pre-1949 educational activities of the Communists are described by Michael Lindsay in his *Notes on Educational Problems in Communist China, 1941–1947,* with supplements on developments in 1948 and 1949 by Marion Menzies, William Paget, and S. B. Thomas (New York, 1950). Rewi Alley, a New Zealander who spent a number of years in interior China working with the

Gung-ho or Industrial Cooperatives during the war against Japan, describes the educational experiment in *Sandan: An Adventure in Creative Education* (Christchurch, New Zealand, 1959).

A not negligible body of material has accumulated on educational development in China since the Communist takeover. Works of a general nature include Lin En-chin, *Educational Changes in China since the Establishment of the People's Republic and Some Steps Leading to Them: A Report* (Philadelphia, Pennsylvania, 1953); Chi Tung-wei, *Education for the Proletariat in Communist China* (Hong Kong, 1954); Theodore H. E. Chen, "New Schools for China" (*Current History*, vol. XXII, June 1952), and a more recent article on "Education and Indoctrination in Communist China" (*Current History*, September 1961); William Benton, "Education in Red China" (*Saturday Review*, July 15, 1961); the chapter on education in C. T. Hu, *et al.*, *China, Its People, Its Society, Its Culture* (New Haven, Connecticut, 1960); and Leo A. Orleans, *Professional Manpower and Education in Communist China* (Washington, D.C., 1960).

On the role and life of students, see Chao Chung and Yang I-fan, *Students in Mainland China* (Hong Kong, 1956); Maria Yen, *The Umbrella Garden: A Picture of Student Life in Red China* (New York, 1954); and the official Communist presentation entitled *Chinese Students*, issued through the Foreign Language Press of Peking by the All-China Students' Federation, 1955.

The important problem of thought reform among the intellectuals is thoroughly analyzed in Theodore H. E. Chen, *Thought Reform of the Chinese Intellectuals* (Hong Kong, 1960). The United States Office of Education has published, in its Comparative Education Series, *Teacher Training in Communist China*, by Theodore H. E. Chen (Washington, D.C., 1961); and *The Agricultural Middle School in Communist China*, by Robert D. Barendsen (Washington, D.C., 1961); and in its Information on Education Around the World Series, a work by Chester Cheng, entitled *Basic Principles Underlying the*

*Chinese Communist Approach to Education* (Washington, D.C., 1961).

Materials on education from mainland China are plentiful, and the more important documents and policy statements have been made available in English through the invaluable service of the United States Consulate General in Hong Kong, in such series as *Current Background* and *Survey of Mainland China Press*. Needless to say, the Peking Foreign Language Press and other government agencies in mainland China publish a variety of materials in English which often contain information on educational development.

# 1: On Practice

## By MAO TSE-TUNG

*This article, written in July 1937, is taken from* Selected Works of Mao Tse-tung *(London: Lawrence and Wishart, 1954), volume 1, pages 282–297. The original introductory note states: "This article was written to expose from the viewpoint of Marxist theory of knowledge such subjectivist mistakes in the Party as doctrinairism and empiricism, especially doctrinairism. As its stress is laid on exposing doctrinaire subjectivism which belittles practice, this article is entitled 'On Practice'. These views were originally presented in a lecture at the Anti-Japanese Military and Political College in Yenan."*

### ON THE RELATION BETWEEN KNOWLEDGE AND PRACTICE—BETWEEN KNOWING AND DOING

To make clear the dialectical-materialist process of knowledge arising from the practice of changing reality—the gradually deepening process of knowledge—a few concrete examples are given below:

In its knowledge of capitalist society in the first period of its practice—the period of machine-smashing and spontaneous struggle—the proletariat, as yet in the stage of perceptual knowledge, only knew the separate aspects and external relations of the various phenomena of capitalism. At that time the proletariat was what we call a "class in itself." But when this class reached the second period of its practice—the period of conscious, organized, economic struggle and political struggle—when through its practice, through its experience gained in long-term struggles, and through its education in Marxist theory, which is a summing-up of these experiences by Marx and Engels according to scientific method, it came to understand the essence of capitalist society, the relations of exploitation between social classes, and its own historical task, and then became a "class for itself."

Similarly with the Chinese people's knowledge of imperialism. The first stage was one of superficial, perceptual knowledge, as shown in the indiscriminate antiforeign struggles of the Movement of the T'aip'ing Heavenly Kingdom, the Boxer Movement, etc. It was only in the second stage that the Chinese people arrived at rational knowledge, when they saw the internal and external contradictions of imperialism, as well as the essence of the oppression and exploitation of China's broad masses by imperialism in alliance with China's compradors and feudal class; such knowledge began only about the time of the May 4 Movement of 1919.

Let us also look at war. If those who direct a war lack war experience, then in the initial stage they will not understand the profound laws for directing a particular war (for example, our Agrarian Revolutionary War of the past ten years). In the initial stage they merely undergo the experience of a good deal of fighting, and what is more, suffer many defeats. But from such experience (of battles won and especially of battles lost), they are able to understand the inner thread of the whole war, namely, the laws governing that particular war, to understand strategy and tactics, and consequently they are able to direct the war with confidence. At such a time, if an inexperienced person takes over the command, he, too, cannot understand the true laws of war until after he has suffered a number of defeats (after he has gained experience).

We often hear the remark made by a comrade when

he has not the courage to accept an assignment: "I have no confidence." Why has he no confidence? Because he has no systematic understanding of the nature and conditions of the work, or because he has had little or even no contact with this kind of work; hence the laws governing it are beyond him. After a detailed analysis of the nature and conditions of the work, he will feel more confident and become willing to do it. If, after doing the work for some time, this person has gained experience in it, and if moreover he is willing to look at things with an open mind and does not consider problems subjectively, one-sidedly, and superficially, he will be able to draw conclusions as to how to proceed with his work and his confidence will be greatly enhanced. Only those are bound to stumble who look at problems subjectively, one-sidedly, and superficially and, on arriving at a place, issue orders or directives in a self-complacent manner without considering the circumstances, without viewing things in their totality (their history and their present situation as a whole), and without coming into contact with the essence of things (their qualities and the internal relations between one thing and another).

Thus the first step in the process of knowledge is contact with the things of the external world; this belongs to the stage of perception. The second step is a synthesis of the data of perception by making a rearrangement or a reconstruction; this belongs to the stage of conception, judgment, and inference. It is only when the perceptual data are extremely rich (not fragmentary or incomplete) and are in correspondence to reality (not illusory) that we can, on the basis of such data, form valid concepts and carry out correct reasoning.

Here two important points must be emphasized. The first, a point which has been mentioned before, but should be repeated here, is the question of the dependence of rational knowledge on perceptual knowledge. The person who thinks that rational knowledge need not be derived from perceptual knowledge is an idealist. In the history of philosophy there is the so-called "rationalist" school which admits only the validity of reason, but not the validity of experience, regarding reason alone as reliable and perceptual experience as unreliable; the mistake of this school consists in turning things upside down. The rational is reliable precisely because it has its source in the perceptual; otherwise it would be like water without a source or a tree without roots, something subjective, spontaneous, and unreliable. As to the sequence in the process of knowledge, perceptual experience comes first; we emphasize the significance of social practice in the process of knowledge precisely because social practice alone can give rise to man's knowledge and start him on the acquisition of perceptual experience from the objective world surrounding him. For a person who shuts his eyes, stops his ears, and totally cuts himself off from the objective world, there can be no knowledge to speak of. Knowledge starts with experience—this is the materialism of the theory of knowledge.

The second point is that knowledge has yet to be deepened, the perceptual stage of knowledge has yet to be developed to the rational stage—this is the dialectics of the theory of knowledge.[1] It would be a repetition of the mistake of "empiricism" in history to hold that knowledge can stop at the lower stage of perception and that perceptual knowledge alone is reliable while rational knowledge is not. This theory errs in failing to recognize that, although the data of perception reflect certain real things of the objective world (I am not speaking here of idealist empiricism which limits experience to so-called introspection), yet they are merely fragmentary and superficial, reflecting things incompletely instead of representing their essence. To reflect a thing fully in its totality, to reflect its essence and its inherent laws, it is necessary, through thinking, to build up a system of concepts and theories by subjecting the abundant perceptual data to a process of remodeling and reconstructing—discarding the crude and selecting the refined, eliminating the false and re-

[1] V. I. Lenin, *Materialism and Empirio-Criticism*, Chapter III, Section 6, p. 146: "For the sake of knowing, one must start to know, to study, on the basis of experience and rise from experience to general knowledge."

taining the true, proceeding from one point to another, and going through the outside into the inside; it is necessary to leap from perceptual knowledge to rational knowledge. Knowledge which is such a reconstruction does not become emptier or less reliable; on the contrary, whatever has been scientifically reconstructed on the basis of practice in the process of knowledge is something which, as Lenin said, reflects objective things more deeply, more truly, more fully. As against this, the vulgar plodders, respecting experience yet despising theory, cannot take a comprehensive view of the entire objective process, lack clear direction and long-range perspective, and are self-complacent with occasional successes and peephole views. Were those persons to direct a revolution, they would lead it up a blind alley.

The dialectical-materialist theory of knowledge is that rational knowledge depends on perceptual knowledge and perceptual knowledge has yet to be developed into rational knowledge. Neither "rationalism" nor "empiricism" in philosophy recognizes the historical or dialectical nature of knowledge, and although each contains an aspect of truth (here I am referring to materialist rationalism and empiricism, not to idealist rationalism and empiricism), both are erroneous in the theory of knowledge as a whole. The dialectical-materialist process of knowledge from the perceptual to the rational applies to a minor process of knowledge (knowing a single thing or task) as well as to a major one (knowing a whole society or a revolution).

But the process of knowledge does not end here. The statement that the dialectical-materialist process of knowledge stops at rational knowledge covers only half the problem. And so far as Marxist philosophy is concerned, it covers only the half that is not particularly important. What Marxist philosophy regards as the most important problem does not lie in understanding the laws of the objective world and thereby becoming capable of explaining it, but in actively changing the world by applying the knowledge of its objective laws. From the Marxist viewpoint, theory is important, and its importance is fully shown in Lenin's statement: "Without a revolutionary theory there can be no revolutionary movement."[2] But Marxism emphasizes the importance of theory precisely and only because it can guide action. If we have a correct theory, but merely prate about it, pigeonhole it, and do not put it into practice, then that theory, however good, has no significance.

Knowledge starts with practice, reaches the theoretical plane via practice, and then has to return to practice. The active function of knowledge not only manifests itself in the active leap from perceptual knowledge to rational knowledge, but also—and this is the more important—in the leap from rational knowledge to revolutionary practice. The knowledge which enables us to grasp the laws of the world must be redirected to the practice of changing the world, that is, it must again be applied in the practice of production, in the practice of the revolutionary class struggle and revolutionary national struggle, as well as in the practice of scientific experimentation. This is the process of testing and developing theory, the continuation of the whole process of knowledge.

The problem of whether theory corresponds to objective reality is not entirely solved in the process of knowledge from the perceptual to the rational as described before, nor can it be completely solved in this way. The only way of solving it completely is to redirect rational knowledge to social practice, to apply theory to practice and see whether it can achieve the anticipated results. Many theories of natural science are considered true, not only because they were so considered when natural scientists originated them, but also because they have been verified in subsequent scientific practice. Similarly, Marxism-Leninism is considered true not only because it was so considered when Marx, Engels, Lenin, and Stalin scientifically formulated it but also because it has been verified in the subsequent practice of revolutionary class struggle and revolutionary national struggle. Dialectical materialism is a universal truth because it is impossible for anyone to get away from it in his practice. The his-

2 V. I. Lenin, *What Is to Be Done?*

tory of human knowledge tells us that the truth of many theories is incorrect, and it is through the test of practice that their incorrectness will be rectified. This is the reason why practice is called the criterion of truth and why "the standpoint of life, of practice, should be first and fundamental in the theory of knowledge." [3] Stalin well said: "Theory becomes aimless if it is not connected with revolutionary practice, just as practice gropes in the dark if its path is not illumined by revolutionary theory." [4]

When we get to this point, is the process of knowledge completed? Our answer is: It is and yet it is not. When man in society devotes himself to the practice of changing a certain objective process at a certain stage of its development (whether a natural or social process), he can, by the reflection of the objective process in his thought and by the functioning of his own subjective activity, advance his knowledge from the perceptual to the rational and bring forth ideas, theories, plans, or programs which on the whole correspond to the laws of that objective process; he then puts these ideas, theories, plans, or programs into practice in the same objective process; and the process of knowledge as regards this concrete process can be considered as completed if, through the practice in that objective process, he can realize his preconceived aim, namely, if he can turn these preconceived ideas, theories, plans, or programs into facts. For example, in the process of changing nature, such as in the realization of an engineering plan, the verification of a scientific hypothesis, the production of a utensil or instrument, the reaping of a crop; or in the process of changing society, such as in the victory of a strike, the victory of a war, the fulfillment of an educational plan—all these can be considered as the realization of preconceived aims. But generally speaking, whether in the practice of changing nature or of changing society, people's original ideas, theories, plans, or programs are seldom realized without any

3 V. I. Lenin, *Materialism and Empirio-Criticism*, Chapter II, Section 6.

4 Joseph Stalin, *Foundations of Leninism*.

change whatever. This is because people engaged in changing reality often suffer from many limitations; they are limited not only by the scientific and technological conditions, but also by the degree of development and revelation of the objective process itself (by the fact that the aspects and essence of the objective process have not yet been fully disclosed). In such a situation, ideas, theories, plans, or programs fail partially or wholly to correspond to reality and are partially and sometimes even wholly changed with the discovery of unforeseen circumstances during practice. That is to say, it does happen that the original ideas, theories, plans, or programs fail partially or wholly to correspond to reality and are partially or entirely incorrect. In many instances, failures have to be repeated several times before erroneous knowledge can be rectified and made to correspond to the laws of the objective process, so that subjective things can be transformed into objective things, viz., the anticipated results can be achieved in practice. But in any case, at such a point, the process of man's knowledge of a certain objective process at a certain stage of its development is regarded as completed.

As regards man's process of knowledge, however, there can be no end to it. As any process, whether in the natural or social world, advances and develops through its internal contradictions and struggles, man's process of knowledge must also advance and develop accordingly. In terms of social movement, not only must a true revolutionary leader be adept at correcting his ideas, theories, plans, or programs when they are found to be erroneous, as we have seen, but he must also, when a certain objective process has already advanced and changed from one stage of development to another, be adept at making himself and all his fellow revolutionaries advance and revise their subjective ideas accordingly, that is to say, he must propose new revolutionary tasks and new working programs corresponding to the changes in the new situation. Situations change very rapidly in a revolutionary period; if the knowledge of revolutionaries does not change rapidly in accordance wth the changed situation, they cannot lead the revolution toward victory.

It often happens, however, that ideas lag behind actual events; this is because man's knowledge is limited by a great many social conditions. We oppose the die-hards in the revolutionary ranks whose ideas, failing to advance with the changing objective circumstances, manifest themselves historically as Right opportunism. These people do not see that the struggles arising from contradictions have already pushed the objective process forward, while their knowledge has stopped at the old stage. This characterizes the ideas of all die-hards. With their ideas divorced from social practice, they cannot serve to guide the chariot wheels of society; they can only trail behind the chariot grumbling that it goes too fast, and endeavor to drag it back and make it go in the opposite direction.

We also oppose the phrase-mongering of the "Leftists." Their ideas are ahead of a given stage of development of the objective process: Some of them regard their fantasies as truth; others, straining to realize at present an ideal which can only be realized in the future, divorce themselves from the practice of the majority of the people at the moment and from the realities of the day and show themselves as adventurists in their actions. Idealism and mechanistic materialism, opportunism and adventurism, are all characterized by a breach between the subjective and the objective, by the separation of knowledge from practice. The Marxist-Leninist theory of knowledge, which is distinguished by its emphasis on social practice as the criterion of scientific truth, cannot but resolutely oppose these incorrect ideologies. The Marxist recognizes that in the absolute, total process of the development of the universe, the development of each concrete process is relative; hence, in the great stream of absolute truth, man's knowledge of the concrete process at each given stage of development is only relatively true. The sum total of innumerable relative truths is the absolute truth.[5]

The development of the objective process is full of

[5] V. I. Lenin, *Materialism and Empirio-Criticism*, Chapter II, Section 5.

contradictions and struggles. The development of the process of man's knowledge is also full of contradictions and struggles. All the dialectical movements of the objective world can sooner or later be reflected in man's knowledge. As the process of emergence, development and disappearance in social practice is infinite, the process of emergence, development and disappearance in human knowledge is also infinite. As the practice directed toward changing objective reality on the basis of definite ideas, theories, plans, or programs develops farther ahead each time, man's knowledge of objective reality likewise becomes deeper each time. The process of change in the objective world will never end, nor will man's knowledge of truth through practice. Marxism-Leninism has in no way summed up all knowledge of truth, but is ceaselessly opening up, through practice, the road to the knowledge of truth. Our conclusion is for the concrete and historical unity of the subjective and the objective, of theory and practice, and of knowing and doing, and against all incorrect ideologies, whether "Right" or "Left," which depart from concrete history. With society developed to its present stage, it is on the shoulders of the proletariat and its party that, from historical necessity, the responsibility for correctly understanding and changing the world has fallen. This process of the practice of changing the world, determined on the basis of scientific knowledge, has already reached a historic moment in the world and in China, a moment of such importance as human history has never before witnessed, i.e., a moment for completely dispelling the darkness in the world and in China and bringing about such a world of light as never existed before.

The struggle of the proletariat and revolutionary people in changing the world consists in achieving the following tasks: remolding the objective world as well as their own subjective world—remolding their faculty of knowing as well as the relations between the subjective world and the objective world. Such a remolding has already been effected in one part of the globe, namely, the Soviet Union. The people there are still expediting this remolding process. The people of China and the rest of the world are either passing, or will pass, through such a remolding process. And the objective world which is to be remolded includes the opponents of remolding, who must undergo a stage of compulsory remolding before they can pass to a stage of conscious remolding. When the whole of mankind consciously remolds itself and changes the world, the era of world communism will dawn.

To discover truth through practice, and through practice to verify and develop truth; to start from perceptual knowledge and actively develop it into rational knowledge; and then, starting from rational knowledge, actively to direct revolutionary practice so as to remold the subjective and the objective world will require practice, knowledge, more practice, more knowledge. The cyclical repetition of this pattern will continue to infinity, and with each cycle, the elevation of the content of practice and knowledge will proceed to a higher level. Such is the whole of the dialectical-materialist theory of knowledge, and such is the dialectical-materialist theory of the unity of knowing and doing.

# 2: How to Be a Good Communist

## By LIU SHAO–CH'I

*Chairman of the People's Republic of China since April 1959, Liu Shao-ch'i has long been regarded as one of the chief theoreticians and party organizers. The following is an excerpt from a booklet of the above title, published by the Foreign Languages Press (Peking, 1951). The publication grew out of a series of lectures given at the Institute of Marxism-Leninism in Yenan in 1939, and the title has also been translated as* On the Training of a Communist Party Member.

Comrades! In order to become the most faithful and best pupils of Marx, Engels, Lenin, and Stalin we need to continue to cultivate all aspects in the course of the long and great revolutionary struggle of the proletariat and the masses of the people. We need to continue to cultivate the theories of Marxism-Leninism and to apply such theories in practice; to cultivate revolutionary strategy and tactics; to cultivate the study and methods of dealing with various problems according to the standpoint and methods of Marxism-Leninism; to cultivate our ideology and moral character; to cultivate Party unity, inner-Party struggle and discipline; to cultivate hard work and the method of work; to cultivate skill in dealing with different kinds of people and in associating with the masses of the people; and to cultivate various kinds of scientific knowledge, and so on. We are all Communist

Party members and so we have a general cultivation in common. But there exists a wide discrepancy today between our Party members. Wide discrepancy exists among us in the level of political consciousness, in work, in position, in cultural level, in experience of struggle, and in social origin. Therefore, in addition to cultivation in general we also need special cultivation for different groups and for individual comrades.

Accordingly, there should be different methods and forms of cultivation. For example, many of our comrades keep diaries in order to have a daily check on their work and thoughts or they write down on small posters their personal defects and what they hope to achieve, and paste them up where they work or live, together with the photographs of persons they look up to, and they ask comrades for criticism and supervision. In ancient China, there were many methods of cultivation. There was Tseng Tze who said: "I reflect on myself three times a day." *The Book of Odes* has it that one should cultivate oneself "as a lapidary cuts and files, carves and polishes." Another method was "to examine oneself by self-reflection" and to "write down some mottoes on the right hand side of one's desk" or "on one's girdle" as daily reminders of rules of personal conduct. The Chinese scholars of the Confucian school had a number of methods for the cultivation of their bodies and minds. Every religion has various methods and forms of cultivation of its own. The "investigation of things, the extension of knowledge, the sincerity of thought, the rectification of the heart, the cultivation of the person, the regulation of the family, the ordering well of the state, and the making tranquil of the whole kingdom" as set forth in *The Great Learning*[1] also mean the same.

All this shows that in achieving progress one must make serious and energetic efforts to carry on self-cultivation and study. However, many of these methods and forms cannot be adopted by us because most of them are

[1] *The Great Learning* is said to be "a Book handed down by the Confucian school, which forms the gate by which beginners enter into virtue."

idealistic, formalistic, abstract, and divorced from social practice. These scholars and religious believers exaggerate the function of subjective initiative, thinking that so long as they keep their general "good intentions" and are devoted to silent prayer they will be able to change the existing state of affairs, change society, and change themselves under conditions separated from social and revolutionary practice. This is, of course, absurd. We cannot cultivate ourselves in this way. We are materialists and our cultivation cannot be separated from practice.

What is important to us is that we must not under any circumstances isolate ourselves from the revolutionary struggles of different kinds of people and of different forms at a given moment and that we must, moreover, sum up historical revolutionary experience and learn humbly from it and put it into practice. That is to say, we must undertake self-cultivation and steel ourselves in the course of our own practice, basing our efforts on the experiences of past revolutionary practice, on the present concrete situation, and on new experiences. Our self-cultivation and steeling are for no other purpose than that of revolutionary practice. That is to say, we must modestly try to understand the standpoint, the method, and the spirit of Marxism-Leninism, and how Marx, Engels, Lenin, and Stalin dealt with people. And having understood these, we should immediately apply them to our own practice, i.e., in our own lives, words, deeds, and work. Moreover, we should stick to them and unreservedly correct and purge everything in our ideology that runs counter to them, thereby strengthening our own proletarian and Communist ideology and qualities. In other words, we must humbly listen to the opinions and criticisms of our comrades and of the masses, carefully study the practical problems in our lives and in our work, and carefully sum up our experiences and the lessons we have learned so as to find an orientation for our own work. In addition, on the basis of all these, we must judge whether we have a correct understanding of Marxism-Leninism, and whether we have correctly applied the method of Marxism-Leninism, discovering our own shortcomings and mistakes and correcting them. At the same time, we must find out in what respects specific conclusions of Marxism-Leninism need to be supplemented, enriched, and developed on the basis of well-digested new experiences. That is to say, we must combine the universal truth of Marxism-Leninism with the concrete practice of the revolution.

These should be the methods of self-cultivation of Communist Party members. We must use the methods of Marxism-Leninism to cultivate ourselves. This kind of cultivation is entirely different from other kinds of cultivation which are idealistic and divorced from social practice.

In this connection, we cannot but oppose certain idle talk and mechanicalism on the question of cultivation and steeling.

First of all, we must oppose and resolutely eliminate one of the biggest evils bequeathed to us by the education and learning in the old society—the separation of theory from practice. In the course of education and study in the old society many people thought that it was unnecessary or even impossible to act on what they had learned. Despite the fact that they read over and over again books by ancient sages, they did things the sages would have been loath to do. Despite the fact that in everything they wrote or said they preached righteousness and morality, they acted like out-and-out robbers and harlots in everything they did. Some "high-ranking officials" issued orders for reading the *Four Books* and the *Five Classics*,[2] yet in their everyday administrative work they ruthlessly extorted exorbitant requisitions, ran amuck with corruption and killing, and did everything against righteousness and morality. Some people read the *Three People's Principles* over and over again and could recite the *Will of Dr. Sun Yat-sen*, yet they oppressed the people, opposed the nations who treated us on an equal footing, and went so far as to compromise with or surrender to the national enemy. Once a scholar of the old school told me himself that the only maxim of Confucius

2 The *Four Books* and the *Five Classics* are nine ancient Chinese classics of philosophy, history, poetry, etc., of the Confucian Canon.

that he could observe was: "To him food can never be too dainty; minced meat can never be too fine," adding that all the rest of the teachings of Confucius he could not observe and had never proposed to observe. Then why did they still want to carry on educational work and study the teachings of the sages? Apart from utilizing them for window-dressing purposes, their objectives were: (1) to use these teachings to oppress the exploited and to use righteousness and morality for the purpose of hood-winking and suppressing the culturally backward people, and (2) to attempt thereby to secure better government jobs, to make money and achieve fame, and to reflect credit on their parents. Apart from these objectives, their actions were not restricted by the sages' teachings. This was the attitude of the "men of letters" and "scholars" of the old society toward the sages they "worshipped." Of course we Communist Party members cannot adopt such an attitude in studying Marxism-Leninism and the excellent and useful teachings bequeathed to us by our ancient sages. We must live up to what we say. We are honest and pure and we cannot deceive ourselves, the people, or our forefathers. This is an outstanding characteristic as well as a great merit of Communist Party members.

Comrades! Is it not possible that the evil legacy of the old society still exerts some influence on us? It does influence us. Among you students there are, of course, none who try to study Marxism for the sake of obtaining higher government posts, making money, or oppressing the exploited. You are studying Marxism for the sake of eliminating the system of exploitation of man by man. However, I cannot guarantee that you have lived up to what you have learned. Are there none among you who think that your thoughts, words, deeds, and lives need not be guided by the principles of Marxism-Leninism and that the principles you have learned need not be put into practice? Again, are there none among you who think that you study Marxism-Leninism and study profound theory in order that you may be promoted, that you may show yourselves off and make yourselves celebrities? I have no guarantee that there are absolutely none among you who think this way. Yet this way of thinking does not conform to Marxism and it represents a gap between Marxist theory and Marxist practice. We have no objection to the study of theory and moreover we must study theory, but what we have learned we must put into practice. We study for the sole purpose of putting into practice what we have learned. It is for the Party and for the victory of the revolution that we study.

For example, you have very often shouted the slogan "Combine theory with practice" but have you combined the theory you have learned with your own practice? Are there not still some among you whose practice is entirely divorced from the principles of Marxism-Leninism? It seems that there are still some among you who understand the combination of theory and practice in the following way: They want comrades working outside the school to come to report on their experiences so as to see how others combine theory with practice, but it is theirs and not yours. I think the fact that you shout the slogan ought to mean that you should combine the theory you study with your own practice. If you do not understand this point in such a way, then what is the use of your shouting the slogan? I will give another example. You have shouted many slogans about the need for steeling yourselves, but are there not some people among you who have shown themselves anything but steeled or have shown that they could not stand up to being steeled when the hour of real test came, when they met with rebuff, or when they were subjected to criticism and punishment, to the pressure of public opinion, and to the correct or incorrect supervision of the great majority of the people? They forgot that a Communist Party member should have a firm will and clear standpoint, etc. They looked dejected, not knowing what to do. Are these not examples of empty talk about steeling and cultivation?

As a matter of fact, the training you receive and the study you make in school are also forms of steeling and cultivation. We are trying to make you into useful cadres and Party workers through training and studying in school, not just to get you to learn only some abstract "theory" and Marxist-Leninist terminology and formulas. Moreover, we want you to cultivate and steel yourselves so as to become cadres who can think correctly, who have a firm will, and who are able to solve in a practical way all kinds of complex problems. However, I have often heard it said that to study in school is not the way to become steeled and that in order to steel and cultivate oneself one must leave school and take up practical work. Comrades! Steeling and cultivation are a lifelong and many-sided task. They are needed everywhere at all times and in relation to all problems. We cannot say that we can undertake steeling and cultivation only at certain times, in certain places in connection with certain matters but not at other times, in other places and in connection with other matters, although we do not deny the fact that Communist Party members should steel and cultivate themselves mainly in the course of the practical struggle of the masses.

In other words, we are opposed to idealism, idle talk, and mechanicalism on the problem of cultivation. We should be able to stand up to being steeled. We should steel ourselves in school, among the masses, and in the struggles both inside and outside the Party. We should study and cultivate ourselves under all circumstances, both of victory and defeat.

### THE RELATION BETWEEN THE STUDY OF MARXIST-LENINIST THEORY AND THE IDEOLOGICAL CULTIVATION OF PARTY MEMBERS

Among our Communist Party members a comparatively prevalent way of thinking is as follows: The firm and pure proletarian Communist standpoint has nothing to do with Communist Party members' understanding and mastery of the theory and method of Marxism-Leninism. They think that although their class standpoint is not very firm and their ideology not very pure (they still retain remnants of the ideology of other classes, and they are still selfish and have material desires and so on), they can nevertheless thoroughly understand and master the theory and method of Marxism-Leninism. Some comrades think that it is possible to thoroughly master the theory and method of Marxism-Leninism merely by means of one's own intellect, ability, and study. Comrades! This way of thinking is wrong.

Mitin, a Soviet philosopher, is quite right when he says:

> Differences in profundity of understanding require a class explanation. For example, at the present time, in the epoch of the decay of capitalism, no matter how talented some ideologist of the bourgeoisie may be, his creative ability, his ability to obtain a penetrating understanding of the laws of development are "constrained" by his class nature, by the conservatism of the class he represents. The inability of the bourgeoisie to foresee the future, determines, narrows the limits and reduces the depth of understanding of the phenomena of social development by bourgeois theoreticians. Notwithstanding all their talents, ideologists of those classes which are passing from the stage of history are not in a position to make really profound scientific conclusions and discoveries. This Marxist truth has been confirmed by the whole history of the development of science and philosophy. (*Dialectical and Historical Materialism,* Part I, page 285, of the Russian edition, edited by M. Mitin. OGIZ, Moscow, 1934.)

Marxism-Leninism is the science of the proletarian revolution. It can be thoroughly understood and mastered only by those who take the proletarian standpoint fully and who adopt the ideals of the proletariat as their own. It is impossible for anyone to thoroughly understand and master the Marxist science of the proletariat, simply by means of his intellect and strenuous study, if he lacks the firm standpoint and pure ideals of the proletariat. This is also an obvious truth. Therefore, in studying the theory and method of Marxism-Leninism today it is necessary that our study proceeds simultaneously with our ideological cultivation and steeling because without the theory and method of Marxism-Leninism, we should have nothing to guide our thoughts and actions, and our ideological cultivation would also be impossible. These two are closely related to each other and are inseparable.

We have often come across some of the best Party members of working-class origin who are less developed in the theory of Marxism-Leninism as compared with those who are making a special study of theory. They would certainly prove less proficient if asked to recite Marxist-Leninist formulas or quotations from Marxist-Leninist works. But when it comes to studying the theory of Marxism-Leninism, quite often their interest is keener and their understanding deeper than those Party members of student origin, provided it is explained to them in words they understand. For example, the chapter in *Capital* dealing with the theory of surplus value is most difficult for some Party members to understand but it is not so difficult for members of working-class origin, because workers fully understand how in the process of production the capitalists calculate wages and working hours, how they make profits, and how they expand production, etc. Therefore, it often happens that they are able to understand Marx's theory of surplus value more completely than other Party members. Especially in observing and dealing with various practical problems, they often prove more apt, more correct, and more in conformity with the principles of Marxism-Leninism than others. Why is this so? It is because they have the firm, pure proletarian and Communist standpoint and ideals, an objective attitude toward things, and in their minds they have no preconceived ideas whatever, no worries about personal problems or about impure matters. Therefore, they can immediately perceive the truth of things and courageously uphold the truth without any hesitation or difficulty.

If among Communist Party members there are still some whose class standpoint is not very clear-cut and firm, whose ideology is not correct and pure, who still retain to some degree remnants of various kinds of ideology, habits, and prejudices of other classes and of the old society, and who still have personal interests and private ends and all kinds of material desires and selfish ideas,

Marxist-Leninist principles and conclusions are certain to clash with all such ideas of theirs when they come to study the theory and method of Marxism-Leninism. In that case, they will either try to overcome their ideas or they will try to distort the principles and conclusions of Marxism-Leninism. They will be unable to penetrate deeply into the essence of Marxism-Leninism, to absorb the quintessence of Marxism-Leninism, which has a distinct class character, and to make this quintessence a weapon of their own because such a weapon has nothing in common with their former class ideology.

Again, when they deal with various practical problems in the course of the proletarian revolution, the solution of these problems in accordance with Marxism-Leninism will often be incompatible with their habits and prejudices and will be in conflict with their personal interests. Under such circumstances, they will show themselves to be petty-minded, irresolute, hesitant, and wavering. They will be unable to deal with problems aptly, correctly, and in an objective way, or to perceive truth without difficulty, or to courageously uphold the truth. They will go so far as to cover up or distort the truth consciously or unconsciously. Comrades! Such cases are by no means rare and strange but are of common occurrence.

Thus we can say: If a Communist Party member lacks the clear-cut, firm, correct, and pure standpoint and ideology of the proletariat, it will be impossible for him to thoroughly understand and master the theory and method of Marxism-Leninism and to make of it a weapon in his own revolutionary struggle.

Therefore, first and foremost in the cultivation of Communist Party members should be ideological cultivation which is the foundation of all other cultivations.

# 3: On the New Democracy

## By MAO TSE-TUNG

*Of all Mao's writings, the treatise* On the New Democracy *has perhaps received the greatest attention and publicity outside China. The selection below is the last section of the original treatise, and appeared under the heading "A National, Scientific and Mass Culture." Completed in January 1940, this work is available in a number of publications, including* Selected Works of Mao Tse-tung *(New York: International Publishers, 1955).*

New democratic culture is national. It opposes imperialist oppression and upholds the dignity and independence of the Chinese nation. It belongs to our own nation, and bears our national characteristics. It unites with the socialist and new-democratic cultures of all other nations, and establishes with them the relations whereby we can absorb something from each other and help each other to develop, and form together the new culture of the world; but it can never unite with the reactionary imperialist culture of any nation, for it is a revolutionary national culture. China should absorb on a large scale the progressive cultures of foreign countries as an ingredient for her own culture; in the past we did not do enough work of this kind. We must absorb whatever we find useful today, not only from the present socialist or new-democratic cultures of other nations, but also from the older cultures of foreign countries, such as those

of the various capitalist countries in the age of enlighten-
ment. However, we must treat these foreign materials as
we do our food, which should be chewed in the mouth,
submitted to the working of the stomach and intestines,
mixed with saliva, gastric juice, and intestinal secretions,
and then separated into essence to be absorbed and waste
matter to be discarded—only thus can food benefit our
body; we should never swallow anything raw or absorb
it uncritically. So-called "wholesale Westernization"[1] is
a mistaken viewpoint. China has suffered a great deal
in the past from the formalist absorption of foreign
things. Likewise, in applying Marxism to China, Chinese
Communists must fully and properly unite the universal
truth of Marxism with the specific practice of the Chinese revolution; that is to say, the truth of Marxism
must be integrated with the characteristics of the nation
and given a definite national form before it can be useful; it must not be applied subjectively as a mere formula. Formula-Marxists are only fooling with Marxism
and the Chinese revolution, and there is no place for
them in the ranks of the Chinese revolution. China's culture should have its own form, namely, a national form.
National in form, new-democratic in content—such is
our new culture today.

New-democratic culture is scientific. It is opposed to
all feudal and superstitious ideas; it stands for seeking
truth from facts; it stands for objective truth and for the
unity between theory and practice. On this point, the
scientific thought of the Chinese proletariat can form
an anti-imperialist, antifeudal, and antisuperstitious
united front with the still progressive bourgeois materialists and natural scientists, but it can never form a united
front with any reactionary idealism. Communists may
form an anti-imperialist and antifeudal united front for
political actions with certain idealists and even with reli-

1 A view advanced by a number of the Chinese bourgeois scholars
completely enslaved by antiquated individualist bourgeois Western
culture. They recommended so-called "wholesale Westernization,"
which means imitating the capitalist countries of Europe and America in everything.

gious followers, but we can never approve of their ideal-ism or religious doctrines. A splendid ancient culture was created during the long period of China's feudal society. To clarify the process of development of this ancient culture, to throw away its feudal dross and to absorb its democratic essence is a necessary condition for the devel-opment of our new national culture and for the increase of our national self-confidence; but we should never ab-sorb anything and everything uncritically. We must sep-arate all the rotten things of the ancient feudal ruling class from the fine ancient popular culture that is more or less democratic and revolutionary in character. As China's present new politics and new economy have de-veloped out of her old politics and old economy, and her new culture has also developed out of her old culture, we must respect our own history and should not cut our-selves adrift from it. However, this respect for history simply means giving history a definite place among the sciences, respecting its dialectical development, but not eulogizing the ancient while disparaging the modern, or praising any noxious feudal element. As to the masses of the people and the young students, the essential thing is to direct them not to look backward, but to look forward.

New-democratic culture belongs to the broad masses, hence it is democratic. It should be in the service of the toiling masses of workers and peasants who constitute more than 90 per cent of the nation's population, and it should gradually become their culture. The knowledge to be imparted to the revolutionary cadres and the knowledge to be imparted to the broad revolutionary masses must be qualitatively different from each other but still also linked to each other; elevation and popu-larization must be distinguished from each other but linked to each other. Revolutionary culture is a power-ful revolutionary weapon for the broad masses of the people. Before the revolution comes, revolutionary cul-ture prepares for it in the ideological field; during the revolution, it is a necessary and important sector in the general revolutionary front. Revolutionary cultural work-ers are the commanders of various ranks on this cultural front. "Without a revolutionary theory, there can be no revolutionary movement,"[2] thus one can see how important the revolutionary cultural movement is to the practical revolutionary movement. And the cultural movement and practical movement are both of a mass character. Therefore all progressive cultural workers should have their own cultural army in the Anti-Japanese War, and this army is the broad mass of the people themselves. A revolutionary cultural worker who does not get close to the people is merely "a general without an army," and his firing power cannot bring the enemy down. For the realization of this aim, our written language must be reformed in certain ways, and our spoken language must be brought close to that of the people; we must know that the people are the inexhaustibly rich source of our revolutionary culture.

National, scientific, and mass culture is the anti-imperialist, antifeudal culture of the broad masses of the people; it is new-democratic culture and the new culture of the Chinese nation.

The combination of new-democratic politics, new-democratic economy, and new-democratic culture is precisely a republic of New Democracy, a republic of China in name and in fact and the new China we want to build.

This New China stands before every Chinese; we should welcome her.

The mast of the ship *New China* is appearing above the horizon; we should clap our hands and hail her.

Raise both your hands: New China is ours!

2 V. I. Lenin, *What Is to Be Done?*

# 4: On the Correct Handling of Contradictions among the People

## By MAO TSE–TUNG

*This is an excerpt from a speech by Mao Tse-tung de-
livered on February 27, 1957, at the Eleventh Enlarged
Session of the Supreme State Conference. After some re-
visions by the author, the text was released by the New
China News Agency and published in pamphlet form.
It has, since its publication, been widely used as a text
for socialist education and represents Mao's views on the
various problems besetting China at that stage of her development. The selection below deals with the question
of intellectuals.*

Contradictions within the ranks of the people in our
country also find expression among our intellectuals.
Several million intellectuals who worked for the old society have come to serve the new society. The question
that now arises is how they can best meet the needs of the
new society and how we can help them do so. This is also
a contradiction among the people.

Most of our intellectuals have made marked progress
during the past seven years. They express themselves in
favor of the socialist system. Many of them are diligently
studying Marxism, and some have become Communists.
Their number, though small, is growing steadily. There
are, of course, still some intellectuals who are skeptical

of socialism or who do not approve of it, but they are in a minority.

China needs as many intellectuals as she can get to carry through the colossal task of socialist construction. We should trust intellectuals who are really willing to serve the cause of socialism, radically improve our relations with them, and help them solve whatever problems that have to be solved, so that they can give full play to their talents. Many of our comrades are not good at getting along with intellectuals. They are stiff with them, lack respect for their work, and interfere in scientific and cultural matters in a way that is uncalled for. We must do away with all such shortcomings.

Our intellectuals have made some progress, but they should not be complacent. They must continue to remold themselves, gradually shed their bourgeois world outlook, and acquire a proletarian, communist world outlook so that they can fully meet the needs of the new society and closely unite with the workers and peasants. This change in world outlook is a fundamental one, and up to now it cannot be said that most of our intellectuals have accomplished it. We hope that they will continue making progress, and, in the course of work and study, gradually acquire a communist world outlook, get a better grasp of Marxism-Leninism, and identify themselves with the workers and peasants. We hope they will not stop halfway, or, what is worse, slip back; for if they do they will find themselves in a blind alley.

Since the social system of our country has changed and the economic basis of bourgeois ideology has in the main been destroyed, it is not only necessary but also possible for large numbers of our intellectuals to change their world outlook. But a thorough change in world outlook takes quite a long time, and we should go about it patiently and not be impetuous. Actually, there are bound to be some who continue to be reluctant, ideologically, to accept Marxism-Leninism and communism. We should not be too exacting in what we expect of them; as long as they comply with the requirements of the state and engage in legitimate pursuits, we should give them opportunities for suitable work.

There has been a falling off recently in ideological and political work among students and intellectuals, and some unhealthy tendencies have appeared. Some people apparently think that there is no longer any need to concern themselves about politics, the future of their motherland, and the ideals of mankind. It seems as if the Marxism that was once all the rage is not so much in fashion now. If this is true, we must improve our ideological and political work.

Both students and intellectuals should study hard. In addition to specialized subjects, they should study Marxism-Leninism, current events, and political affairs in order to progress both ideologically and politically. Not to have a correct political point of view is like having no soul. Ideological remolding in the past was necessary and has yielded positive results. But it was carried on in a somewhat rough and ready way and the feelings of some people were hurt—this was not good. We must avoid such shortcomings in the future. All departments and organizations concerned should take up their responsibilities with regard to ideological and political work. This applies to the Communist Party, the Youth League, government departments responsible for this work, and especially the heads of educational institutions and teachers.

Our educational policy must enable everyone who gets an education to develop morally, intellectually, and physically and become cultured, socialist-minded workers. We must spread the idea of building our country through hard work and thrift. We must see to it that all our young people understand that ours is still a very poor country, that we cannot change this situation radically in a short time, and that only through the united hands can our country be made strong and prosperous within a period of several decades. It is true that the establishment of our socialist system has opened the road leading to the ideal state of the future, but we must work hard, very hard indeed, if we are to make that ideal a reality. Some of our young people think that everything ought to be perfect once a socialist society is established and that they should be able to enjoy a happy life, ready-made, without working for it. This is unrealistic.

# 5: In Refutation of an Antisocialist Scientific Program

## By KUO MO–JO

*Kuo Mo-jo, historian, poet, novelist, and President of the Chinese Academy of Sciences, is perhaps one of the most versatile literary figures in modern China. In this speech to the Fourth Session of the First National People's Congress in July 1957, Kuo explains the meaning of scientism as a principle of education. The speech was printed in the* Jen Min Jih Pao *of Peking on July 6, 1957, and an English translation can be found in* Current Background *(No. 467, U.S. Consulate General, Hong Kong).*

In his "Report on Government Work," Premier Chou En-lai has summed up in all respects the great achievements and rich experience gained in our country during the past year, sternly and justly refuted the various erroneous views of the rightists, and answered some questions on scientific work in which our scientists are generally interested. I fully endorse Premier Chou En-lai's report and the other reports.

Permit me to make a few supplementary remarks on the question of scientific work.

Since the liberation, science has gradually begun to thrive in our country. Our scientists are eager to make progress and are quite willing to devote themselves to the service of the great cause of national construction.

Following the call of the Chinese Communist Party Central Committee last year to "march on science," our scientists have shown unprecedented enthusiasm in participating in the socialist construction. Many of them have taken part in the making of the long-term plan for scientific development and, moreover, have done a large amount of research work. Meanwhile, further attention and support have been given to our scientific work by the Chinese Academy of Sciences, the Ministry of Higher Education, other government departments, and local party and government leadership organs, thus enabling our scientific enterprises to make remarkable progress within a very short time.

While our science is taking big strides forward, many problems and difficulties will naturally arise which need our solution. In his report "On the Correct Handling of Contradictions Among the People" (see pages 80–83) delivered at a recent session of the Supreme State Conference, Chairman Mao Tse-tung has given our scientists a powerful ideological weapon for the correct solution of these problems. In connection with the study of Chairman Mao Tse-tung's report, the Chinese Academy of Sciences and other scientific institutions held a series of forums in April in which many scientists took part. Then, late in May, the Chinese Academy of Sciences held the second plenary conference of its Academic Departments Committee, and in the middle of June the Fourth Enlarged Meeting of the Scientific Planning Committee of the State Council was held. At these meetings our scientists eagerly discussed ways and means for further developing our science and put forward a large amount of constructive criticisms and suggestions concerning our scientific work. All these will undoubtedly do much good in overcoming our faults and improving our work.

Naturally, it is impossible to imagine that all the criticisms and suggestions put forward are correct. As a matter of fact, certain mistaken views and ideas still exist in varying degrees of intensity among our scientists. For instance, we think that under the concrete conditions in our country scientific work should proceed according to plan and under a certain leadership, and that scientific research should be based on the policy of combining the needs of national construction with the special aptitudes and interests of individual scientists and on the principle of subservience of scientific research to the requirements of the state. But some scientists think that they can do without plans and leadership and that scientific research need not be geared to the many kinds of constructive work going on in the country. They stand for absolute individual freedom in scientific research and want to carry on scientific research purely for the sake of science. The genesis of these mistaken views has subjective as well as objective roots. Some of our scientists are not yet accustomed to the principles of scientific work under the socialist system. Others do not understand quite well the practical situation of our scientific work, and do not know how to deal correctly with the problems that have arisen in the course of their work. It is no wonder, therefore, that some mistaken views have emerged. As everybody knows, the Party and the government, together with the scientists, are taking correct and effective measures for solving some of the ideological and practical problems that have recently appeared in connection with scientific work, so as to speed up the forward progress of our sciences.

But rightists of the bourgeois class, taking advantage of the erroneous views of some of the scientists, have launched a furious attack on the Party and the government in an attempt to seize the leadership for scientific work and to lead the scientists away from the socialist road. The memorandum, "Some Views on the Question of the Scientific System of Our Country," published in the name of the Provisional Group on Scientific Planning of the Central Committee of the Democratic League and at the instance of Chang Po-chun and others, is a confession of this vicious attempt of the rightists of the bourgeois class.

The memorandum puts forward the slogan, "Protect the Scientists!" Obviously it is trying to create the impression that the scientists in our country are being intimidated or persecuted, and that they need "protection." Some one has actually said, "A calamity has befallen the Chinese intellectuals since the liberation." The objectives of the rightists in making such an extravagant statement in complete disregard of the facts are to estrange the scientists from the Party and the government and to lure them onto false roads.

Most of our scientists, speaking from their personal experience, have expressed unbiased views on the matter. They feel deeply the Party's and government's respect and concern for, and their confidence in, the scientists themselves, and they know that the Party and the government are constantly doing their best to produce the best possible conditions for the scientists to do their work. They believe that the progress made by Chinese science under the leadership of the Party and the government in the few years since the liberation is greater than that made in the past decades or even centuries. And that is true.

Take, for instance, the funds made available for scientific enterprises. Using the appropriation for the Chinese Academy of Sciences in 1950 as the base figure, the appropriation for 1953 was more than ten times that amount, and that for 1956 was more than twenty times the 1950 figure. The absolute amount for 1956 was ¥66,-740,000. Of the appropriations allotted to institutions of higher learning for scientific research by the Ministry of Higher Education, using the figure for 1955 as the base, the 1956 figure was more than eight times and that for 1957 more than thirteen times as much. The absolute figure for 1957 was ¥10,000,000.

Again, take the imports of foreign scientific books and publications. In 1956, foreign-exchange allocations for books and publications from capitalist countries alone amounted to £1,800,000 sterling. The allocations for 1957 are somewhat lower, but still reach £1,500,000 sterling. These figures for imports of foreign publications are larger than those of Japan, India, or the Soviet Union. Taking a single research institute as an example, the Chemical Research Department of the former Peiping

Research Institute had about 2,000 books and 34 different magazines, while the newly established Chemical Research Institute has 14,800 books and 825 magazines.

In the face of these figures, no honest scientist would deny that the Party and the government have done a great deal to ensure good working conditions for the scientists.

Of course, our work of national construction is complicated and heavy, and with our lack of trained personnel, the absence of a sound foundation, and insufficient funds, we cannot as yet do everything to please everyone in the way of ensuring good working conditions for our scientists. We still have many faults, mistakes, and deficiencies which we should try to overcome and correct. In fact, overcoming and correcting these faults and deficiencies is treated as a regular and important task by the Scientific Planning Committee of the State Council, which has already done a great deal in this respect. This situation is known to the rightists, but, deliberately ignoring the facts and assuming a charitable and compassionate attitude, they have been crying, "Protect the scientists!" Is not their intention obvious?

The memorandum prepared by the Provisional Group on Scientific Planning of the Central Committee of the Democratic League is a thoroughly anti-Party, antisocialist program for scientific work.

On the question of organization and leadership of scientific work, the memorandum contains suggestions diametrically opposed to the policy of the Party and the government. This policy is that scientific research should serve the needs of socialist construction, but the memorandum makes no reference whatever to this point. Another point of the policy of the Party and the government is that scientific research should be done according to plan, that there should be "development of the more important branches, with adequate care taken of the rest." The memorandum, however, suggests dispensing with plans or the need for selection of important branches for development, and favors decentralization and laissez-faire policy toward scientific research. It is also the policy of the Party and the government that unified academic leadership for scientific research is necessary, that a "locomotive" is needed for drawing the train of scientific work forward. The memorandum suggests doing without unified academic leadership or any "locomotive."

The basic feature of the socialist character of our scientific work is the subservience of our scientific research to socialist construction. It is the basic feature that distinguishes our scientific work from scientific work in any capitalist country. This is understood by all patriotic scientists and they are willing to work accordingly. The rightists, on the other hand, attempt to lure the scientists away from the needs of the construction of the nation, their object being to change radically the socialist character of our scientific work.

To meet the needs of our national construction, we must, on the existing basis of our scientific work, adequately concentrate our efforts according to plan on the more important branches of work, cooperate more closely with one another, and develop our scientific work rapidly, thoroughly changing the situation where our scientific work is ill-adapted to the needs of our national construction, so that our scientific research work may play its appointed role in the socialist construction. But the memorandum suggests that all "research work" and "funds" for research work should be adapted to "the individual needs of the existing personnel," that is to say, it opposes the development of the more important branches, the necessary concentration, and the expansion of the new branches and organs. It wants those scientists who have changed their fields in obedience to the needs of the state to return to "their former domains of research," that is to say, it opposes the employment of scientists in new, important areas where their services are needed by the state. The rightists oppose the measures taken by the Party and the government and advocate decentralization and free development of scientific research because they do not want our science to adapt itself to the needs of the state or to contribute what it can toward our national construction.

The memorandum opposes in particular unified academic leadership for scientific work—the "locomotive" to scientific work. We should all know that the ability to organize the nation's scientific forces into a unified group capable of undertaking great tasks is a concrete indication of the superiority of the socialist system in the development of science, and that such ability is denied to countries under the capitalist system. The practice of scientific work in our country in the past several years has proved that, in order to lead and direct such a unified scientific force, a unified leadership, a "locomotive," is necessary. In his report on the problem of intellectuals last year, Premier Chou En-lai correctly noted this point. The point was reaffirmed at the recent Fourth Enlarged Meeting of the Scientific Planning Committee of the State Council. The rightists declare that the determination of such a "locomotive" is a "subjective predetermination." They advocate independence for scientific enterprises, which in practice would lead our scientific work into an anarchic state.

The result of opposition to the subservience of science to socialist construction, opposition to the development of scientific work according to plan and in the more important branches, and opposition to unified leadership for scientific work would be to prevent us from making full use of the superiority of the socialist system in the development of our science, and would make our scientific work remain indefinitely where it is—in a backward position. I do not believe that the majority of our scientists would agree with such retrogressive and perverse views of the rightists.

With regard to the question of training new forces of science, the rightists suggest that "equal treatment be given to the people so far as educational opportunities are concerned," and declare accusingly: "In the admission of students into institutions of higher learning, promotion of students to higher classes, and selection of students for research fellowships and for study abroad, there has been deviation in the past in overemphasizing political conditions." They try to bait our youth with the false concept of "equality" of the bourgeois class in the hope of stirring up discontent among some of them against the Party and the government.

It is true that in the regulations governing the entrance examination of institutions of higher learning, preference is given to five classes of candidates when their results are the same as those returned by other classes of candidates. The five classes of candidates are: (1) students of the national minorities; (2) overseas Chinese students and students from Hong Kong and Macau; (3) workers and peasants, graduates of rapid-course middle schools for workers and peasants of the current year, and worker and peasant cadres; (4) demobilized servicemen on construction jobs or servicemen on civilian jobs; and (5) children of revolutionary martyrs.

Can the privilege given to these five classes of candidates be called unequal? Certainly not. If they are given "equal treatment" with the rest, then there would be real injustice. Take the worker and peasant students, for instance. We all know that under the reactionary rule in the old China, the children of peasants and workers were deprived of their right to education, particularly higher education. Now that the reactionary rule is overthrown, should we not do what we can to change this unreasonable and unjust state of affairs? It should be pointed out that up to now and in this respect we have not yet completely eliminated the injustice left by the old society. Let me cite some percentages to illustrate this point.

Of the total number of students in institutions of higher learning in September 1956, only 34.29 per cent were worker-peasant students. In the same period only 17.46 per cent of the research fellows in these institutions were from worker-peasant families. The percentage of research fellows from these families in the Chinese Academy of Sciences is even smaller at present, being only 5.92. According to data made available by the Preparatory Class for Students Selected for Study in the Soviet Union for the period 1952 to 1956, only 30.1 per cent of the students sent to the Soviet Union for advanced studies were from worker-peasant families. These percentages tell us that only a small part of the young scientific cadres now being trained and brought up by the state have come from worker-peasant families, while the majority have come from bourgeois and landlord families. Yet under these circumstances the rightists still shout their slogan of "equal treatment." It is not obvious that their object is deceptive and inflammatory?

As for students from the national minorities, they too were deprived of their right to higher education under the old reactionary regime. I need not dwell on the necessity of taking special care of overseas Chinese students and students from Hong Kong and Macau who have returned to the motherland for advanced studies, and of the children of the revolutionary martyrs who laid down their lives for the cause of the revolution.

The rightists also charge provocatively that in the selection of youth for training as scientific cadres, members of the Communist Party and the Young Communist League enjoy "special privileges." The charge has its ideological background in the slogan of "equal treatment." Actually it is openly anti-Party and antisocialist. The rightists put it mildly by charging that "political conditions are overemphasized." I think that there can be no concession on this point. In the selection of youth for training as scientific cadres we must insist on the political qualifications. That is a point on which we must remain absolutely unshakable. What the state needs is trained personnel for socialist construction. As many as possible of the members of the Communist Party and the Young Communist League should be selected for training if they meet the requirements, including political as well as academic requirements. From our point of view, the more Communists and Young League members the better, but that is bad from the point of view of the rightists of the bourgeois class. Their effort to bar as many as possible of the Communists and members of the Communist League from scientific training is determined by the essential nature of their class. The object of their discrimination against workers and peasants, Communists and members of the Young Communist League is to alter the class composition and political quality of our future scientific-technical force. The rightists are trying to make a subtle substitution.

The Party and the government do not discriminate against youth who do not come from worker-peasant families and who do not belong to either the Communist Party or the Young Communist League, and are not trying to exclude them from scientific training, but on the contrary are showering on them the same affectionate care and giving them the best possible training. Take the research fellows at present in the Chinese Academy of Sciences, for instance: 4.14 per cent are from bourgeois or landlord families, and 37.9 per cent belong to neither the Communist Party nor the Communist Youth League. Humans are capable of ideological reform. If they are willing, all students who do not come from worker-peasant families and who do not belong to either the Communist Party or the Young Communist League can become specialists loyal to the cause of socialism and, like the children of workers and peasants and members of the Communist Party or the Young Communist League, can contribute their share to the work of the state.

With regard to social sciences, the memorandum suggests that "first of all the attitude of the bourgeois class toward the social sciences should be changed" and then these social sciences of the bourgeois class should be "restored." What does that mean? It amounts to a demand that we develop first of all the social sciences not of Marxism but of the bourgeois class. Is such a suggestion acceptable?

Social sciences have a clearly defined class character. The so-called social sciences of the bourgeois class reflect the economic and political system of the bourgeois class and serve the interests of that class. For a long time the bourgeois class has established various kinds of so-called social sciences, including "economics," "politics," and "sociology," but owing to the historical restrictions of the bourgeois class and basing its actions on the narrow interests of that class, it has never been really able to explain scientifically the laws of development of social history or to solve the complicated social problems. Fundamentally speaking, therefore, the so-called social sciences of the bourgeois class are not really scientific. It was in the hands of Marx and Engels that the study of human history and social phenomena began to become a real science. Marx and Engels brought about a revolution in social science. Reversing the idealistic and metaphysical points of view of the bourgeois scholars, Marx and Engels regarded the phenomena of social-economic development as a natural historical process, succeeded in isolating the area of production from all other social relationships, and made it the determining factor of these relationships. Thus they laid the foundation for real social sciences.

Since the liberation, we have made great progress in social sciences. The ranks of Marxist social scientists in China have swollen greatly since the liberation. This is because many of our social scientists, having gone through several great socialist reform movements after the victory of the revolution, particularly the ideological reform movement of the intellectuals and the critical movement against bourgeois idealism, have gradually discarded their former bourgeois viewpoints and arisen from all sides. Thus our research work in social sciences has taken the correct direction of Marxism. Of course, the present development of social sciences in our country is still lagging far behind the needs of our national construction. Serious weaknesses still exist in our research work in social sciences. The basic weakness is that there are too few in the ranks of our social scientists who can really and creatively apply Marxism to their research. In the struggle against the idealism of the bourgeois class we have not come out strong enough. In my view, therefore, the first thing to do to develop social sciences should be to continue expanding our Marxist forces of social science and raising Marxism to a higher level, instead of develop-

ing the social sciences of the bourgeois class. The suggestion to "restore" the bourgeois social sciences amounts to
turning back the clock and in fact opposes study of social sciences by Marxist method. If this suggestion is
adopted and acted upon, the result would be a weakening of Marxist ideological leadership and a resurgence
and reburgeoning of bourgeois idealism. That, of course,
would be contrary to the wishes of the majority of our
social scientists and to the direction of our socialist
construction.

"Someone" has been quoted in the memorandum as
having said that "social sciences in a socialist society must
begin from scratch, as there is nothing to inherit." That
is a completely unfounded lie. Marxists have always advocated the retention of all cultural heritage that is good.
Exceptionally clear direction on that point has been
given in many of the important works of Chairman Mao
Tse-tung and in many important documents of the Chinese Communist Party. As a matter of fact, most social
scientists hold cultural heritage in high esteem. Only
those nihilists called "troglodytes" would stand for rejection of all cultural heritage. Marxism itself is a summation of historical knowledge. Anyone who has read
Lenin's famous thesis, "The Three Sources and Three
Component Parts of Marxism" (*Selected Works of Lenin,*
Chinese version, volume 1, pages 69 to 74) would know
this perfectly. The "starting from scratch" theory is only
a furtive arrow shot by the rightists.

Of course, a difference in principle exists between certain people and us on the question of cultural heritage.
Some people would regard the cultural heritage of the
bourgeois class as something sacred and would accept it
in its entirety or would have it simply "restored." We on
the other hand take a critical attitude, and would carefully assimilate only that part that is positive and beneficial. There is one prerequisite for critical acceptance of
cultural heritage, and that is possession of the ideological
weapon of Marxism. Without Marxism, we shall be without our ability to criticize, and shall be unable to take
only what is good. We want to point out unequivocally

that the rightist stand on this point is diametrically opposed to ours.

It may be seen from the analysis above that the "views"
contained in the memorandum of the Provisional Group
on Scientific Planning of the Central Committee of the
Democratic League is in fact an antisocialist, bourgeois
program for scientific work. It is not an isolated document, but forms part of the plot of Chang Po-chun and
other rightists to seize first of all leadership for cultural-
educational work and then state leadership. For the purpose of seizing the leadership of cultural-educational
work, Chang Po-chun and the other rightists have intensified the activities of the "Group on Scientific Planning"
and the "Group on the Party Committee System in Institutions of Higher Learning" of the four provisional work
groups set up within the Democratic League. In publishing the memorandum, "Some Views," the *Kuang
Ming Jih Pao* also published a short editorial in which
the "views" were hailed as having "opened a new road
toward mutual supervision." What a "new road" toward
restoration of capitalism! It appears that "Some Views"
is in fact the first batch of goods turned out by Chang
Po-chun's "Political Planning Board."

Now that the plot is exposed and the truth is known,
the dream of the rightists to win over a large number of
scientists has been shattered. Facts have shown that the
rightists are necessarily complete subjectivists. They have
overestimated themselves and underestimated the masses.
That is their undoing.

Most of the Chinese scientists are patriotic and willing
to serve the cause of socialist construction. Only a few
would allow themselves to be exploited and directed by
the rightists. It is these few who have been crying "Protect the scientists" who in my opinion should take steps
to protect themselves. They should wake up at once,
thoroughly settle accounts with their own thoughts, dis-
tinguish friend from enemy and right from wrong, and,
standing on the side of the overwhelming majority of
their fellow scientists, resolutely draw the line between
themselves and the rightists. In behalf of our scientists

I wish to make a statement which may be regarded as taking an oath and with which I believe our scientists will agree: We Chinese scientists will persevere indefinitely in voluntary and self-conscious ideological reform and, in the determined struggle against the rightists, further raise the level of our own political thought, rally closer around the Party and the government, and continue to go forward along the road to socialism.

# 6: Actively Carry Out the Reform of the School System to Bring About Greater, Faster, Better, and More Economical Results in the Development of Education

## By YANG HSIU–FENG

*This speech by Yang Hsiu-feng, Minister of Education of the People's Republic of China, was delivered at the Second Session of the Second National People's Congress, April 1960. The English text is taken from* Current Background *(No. 623, U.S. Consulate General, Hong Kong).*

### I

Since 1958, when the Chinese Communist Party Central Committee and the State Council issued the "Directive on Education Work," and stimulated by the successes of the general line, the tremendous forward leaps, and the people's commune campaign, and under conditions of greatly strengthened leadership of the Party, we have fully carried out the educational policy of the Party, enormously developed our educational program, carried out a thoroughgoing revolution, and fulfilled the targets provided in the Second Five-Year Plan three years ahead of schedule.

By 1959 the number of students enrolled in institutions of higher education reached 810,000. This, plus the 300,000 part-time students attending institutions of higher education, has surpassed the target of 850,000. Students full-time in middle schools of all categories amounted to 12.9 million, overfulfilling the target in the Second Five-Year Plan. The number of elementary school students amounted to 90 million, fulfilling the target, and included approximately 87 per cent of the school-age children in China. Compared with the last year of the First Five-Year Plan, 1957, the number of students studying in institutions of higher education in 1959 showed an increase of 87 per cent; in middle schools of all categories, an increase of 82 per cent; and in elementary schools, an increase of 42 per cent.

In the past two years, 60 million persons have lifted themselves from the realm of the illiterate. Tremendous strides have been taken in child education. The minority nationality areas have also greatly developed their education. In the case of Sinkiang, the number of students studying in higher institutions, and in middle and elementary schools, has increased to more than 950,000, or one-fifth of the total population of the entire region. More than 50 per cent of the adults are attending literacy classes and spare-time schools of different levels.

The development of our education in the past two years and more is characterized by the following features:

1. The number of schools has greatly increased. Further, the distribution of schools is more in keeping with the demands for the development of our national economy. Since 1958 the newly established schools have actively streamlined their operational setup and rapidly raised their educational standards.

2. Progress has been made in the setting up of half-day schools. The half-day agricultural schools—including other rural vocational schools—established in 1958 have now taken root in rural areas. We now have more than 30,000 agricultural middle schools with an enrollment of 2.96 million students. The great increase in the number of half-day middle schools in urban and rural areas will enable our country to extend junior middle school education rapidly to all youth of the appropriate age.

3.   Spare-time education for workers and peasants has developed rapidly. Because of the forward-leaping development of industrial and agricultural production, and particularly because of the vigorous progress made in the nationwide technical innovation and technical revolution campaign in the past several months, a surging spare-time study movement has developed among the masses of workers and peasants. By now, approximately 150 million workers and peasants are attending literacy classes and spare-time schools at various levels. Great improvement has been recorded in spare-time education with regard to curricula and the teaching methods.

Important experience has been gained in the elimination of illiteracy with the adoption of the phonetic teaching method. The rapid development of spare-time education in China has considerably speeded up the progress of the revolution to improve the cultural standards of our laboring people.

What about educational standards during the great development? Educational standards have been raised rather than lowered. In some respects, the standards have been raised to considerably higher levels.

Of first and foremost importance is the change in the ideological outlook of teachers and students. In the past two years, following the continual progress and development in the educational revolution, the advance in social practice, and the education program on the general line centering on the study of the documents of the eighth plenary session of the eighth Chinese Communist Party Central Committee, the great masses of teachers and students have raised their socialist and communist consciousness to much higher levels. New communist moral standards are being adopted. Through labor training (contact with the masses of workers and peasants), the teachers and students have strengthened their labor and mass viewpoints and have cultivated class feelings identical with those of the laboring people. At present, a large-scale mass campaign is being carried out among the teachers and students in the study of Mao Tse-tung's works. This marks a new upsurge in Marxist-Leninist education.

Productive labor has taken root in our schools. In the first half of 1959, in compliance with a directive from the CCP Central Committee and the State Council, the full-time schools at the various levels completely rearranged their educational programs covering curricula, productive labor, and the livelihood of the students. The schools have not only gradually established and consolidated their productive labor bases, but have also established normal relations with outside factories, mines, enterprises, farms, and people's communes in order to carry out productive labor on a regular basis.

In the institutions of higher education, coordination between teaching, productive labor, and scientific research has been developed and strengthened. As a result, these three fields have promoted one another and the educational standards have improved in accordance with the mass line.

In 1959, higher educational institutions very successfully carried out their scientific research with emphasis on the policy of placing politics in command, advancing the interests of socialist construction, making more concentrated efforts on research, coordinating more closely with reality, and, particularly, adhering to the mass line. The vigorous development of scientific research in institutions of higher education has lent forceful support to production and construction, enabled it to play its role as an important branch in the science program of the state, enriched the curricula of the institutions concerned, and promoted the elevation of pedagogical standards. Through their participation in scientific research, productive labor, actual practice, engineering tasks which include surveying, designing, and construction operations, academic criticizing practices, social investigations, and basic-level operations, large numbers of students have raised their academic, political, and ideological levels, and their ability to work independently. While in the past it was unthinkable for students to publish books, participate in scientific research work in the most advanced fields, and produce new products, these things are not uncommon today.

In the past year, the middle and elementary schools have universally raised their standards. The students have improved their basic knowledge, fluency in languages, adeptness in mathematics, working habits, and health conditions.

All this shows that our schools have continually raised their educational standards in ideology, knowledge, and physical culture in general, and in some individual branches of education in particular. The fact that our national economy has made continual forward leaps in its development in the past two years has smashed to bits the rightist-inclined opportunists' attacks on the general line, the tremendous forward leaps, and the people's communes. Similarly, the great success in education has proved the complete correctness of the Party's policy on education.

Those who thought that it is possible to achieve greater and faster but not better and more economical results in education, that it "confuses matters" to mobilize the entire Party and all the people to set up large numbers of schools on a highly flexible basis, that it is "penny wise, pound foolish" for the teachers and students to participate in productive labor and thus lower their educational standards, are completely wrong.

Although we have achieved tremendous successes in our educational work, it still does not satisfy the demands of the state for the rapid development of socialist construction. The present very favorable situation for technical innovation, technical revolution, and the development of people's communes has posed a set of new demands on education.

Faced with this new development and these new tasks, it has become most urgent for us to further extend the general line of the Party on socialist construction, the educational policy of the Party, and the work of developing our education program with greater, faster, better, and more economical results. To do so, we should adopt the spirit of the permanent revolution in improving and reforming all fields, particularly in reforming our middle and elementary schools.

## II

Since the founding of our country, we have continually carried out the reform of the school system in our full-time schools. Generally speaking, we have achieved better results in the reform of our higher education and vocational education, although there are still many problems to be solved. With regard to general education, although we have also achieved much success in its reform, we have not yet carried out the necessary radical reforms in the school system, the curricula, and pedagogical methods in order to satisfy the demands of the state for the development of socialist construction. A serious situation characterized by smaller, slower, poorer, and less economical results still exists in these major fields of our education program.

What are the most serious conditions contributing to smaller, slower, poorer, and less economical results in middle and elementary school education today? They are the unnecessarily long period of schooling—twelve years —characterized by the division of elementary and middle school education into four sections, the inclusion of too many courses, the lack of emphasis on the relatively more important courses, and poor selection in the contents of the curricula—all of which adversely affect the mastery of the most important courses by the students. Much of the mathematics, physics, and chemistry now taught in middle schools is old stuff from the nineteenth century which in no way represents the science and technology of today. This backward situation is not in harmony with the socialist construction program being carried out in our country, nor with the development of the intelligence of our youth.

There are also many other problems in our school system and pedagogical methods which cause our general educational program to achieve smaller, slower, poorer, and less economical results. To satisfy the needs of various quarters for socialist construction, it is necessary to surmount this situation quickly by reforming our school system.

Since 1958, in compliance with the "Directive on Education" issued by the Communist Chinese Party Central Committee and the State Council, the various localities have carried out many experiments to reform our school system. Recently, general discussions were held among educational personnel. The experiments and the views advanced in the discussion show that the number of years spent in middle and elementary schools should and can be reduced. Not only that, but after reducing the number of school years, the educational standards can be raised to an appropriate level. The experiments carried out in some localities show that the implementation of the five-year unified elementary school system can bring the standards of the graduates up to that of graduates of the six-year system, or even higher levels.

A number of localities haxe experimented in the implementation of the ten-year unified middle and elementary school education system. Some have advocated adopting the five-year unified middle school educational system or the system of having three years for the junior middle school and two years for the senior middle school. The Peking Normal University stands for the adoption of the nine-year unified middle and elementary school educational system. All these experiments and views indicate that the standards of the middle school graduates under the new systems would be raised to the level of present college freshmen. In addition to the above, there are many other experiments and views in the various localities. The central problem in educational reform lies in reform of the curricula, the school system, materials, and teaching methods.

Highlights of the ways, means, and ideas adopted by the various sections on the reform of the school system are as follows:

1. Transfer some of the present courses in colleges,

middle schools, and elementary schools to suitable lower grades. For example, basic courses such as mathematics, physics, and chemistry, now being taught in natural science, engineering, agricultural, and medical colleges, may be transferred to senior middle schools; all the arithmetic courses and simple algebraic equations now being taught in junior middle schools can be transferred to elementary schools.

2. Merge some courses, condense some courses, and reduce the redundancy of some courses. For instance, the history, geography, and natural science courses in elementary schools can be merged to become the common knowledge course; the Chinese geography, foreign geography, and economic geography courses in middle schools can be merged to become the geography course. The contents of history and geography courses in middle schools should be thoroughly revised and streamlined to cut down redundancy.

3. Reform materials and raise their standards. Outdated and insignificant materials should be discarded and materials on modern sciences, technology, and production should be increased and raised to higher levels. For instance, analytic geometry, and differential and integral calculus should be added to the mathematics course in senior middle schools; the theory of semiconductors should be added to and more advanced basic knowledge on nuclear physics should be included in the physics course in senior middle schools; knowledge of rare elements should be added to and more advanced basic knowledge on high molecular compounds should be included in the chemistry course in senior middle schools.

4. Improve teaching methods. The lecture hours and the hours for secondary courses should be suitably reduced and extracurricular reading, homework, and assistance from teachers should be increased. Lectures should be given with emphasis on major points, which should be explained thoroughly at an advanced level. Examinations should be conducted on a regular basis

in the major courses, and on an optional basis in the others. In the latter case, attention should be paid to the day-to-day improvement by the students.

On the basis of our study and analysis of the prevailing courses and curricular materials, and judging from the initial results obtained in experiments, I hold that the aforementioned hypotheses and measures are based on solid ground. If we carry out our work properly, we can definitely reduce the school years and raise the standards of our students.

We can draw this conclusion because, first and foremost, by suitably streamlining and merging some courses and making a great effort to revise curricular materials and improve teaching methods, we shall enable the students to save much time for concentrating on their main subjects.

Students in full-time middle and elementary schools should study languages—including Chinese and foreign languages—and mathematics properly. These branches of knowledge are the basic tools to be mastered by our students. After mastering languages and mathematics, it will be relatively easy to master other branches of knowledge.

Second, the great masses of our teachers have raised their consciousness for advancing the interests of socialist construction enormously. Under the leadership of the CCP committees concerned, the teachers of different subjects are able to intensify their communist cooperation, coordinate their work, actively improve curricular materials and teaching methods, suitably reduce their lecture hours, and strengthen their extracurricular assistance to students. As a result, greater successes will be achieved by the students in their study when compared to the prevailing system of spending more time listening to lectures than in independent study.

Third, our socialist society has opened a gigantic universe for the over-all development of our children and youth. By participating in productive labor and social and political activities, they have gained much more knowledge than they had before. As a result, the prevailing curricular materials have long been unable to satisfy their demands. For this reason, it is absolutely necessary and possible to raise the standards of the various courses in middle and elementary schools suitably.

In carrying out the reform of the system in middle and elementary schools, it is necessary to increase working hours accordingly. This is because the coordination of education with productive labor is the central task in the educational revolution and is the fundamental way to train all-round new hands. We must not neglect labor at any time.

In the past, because of restrictive labor conditions and long class hours, it was impossible to set aside much time for the students to participate in physical labor. In the future, after tightening control over class hours and after improving and intensifying pedagogical work, it will become possible to increase the students' working hours. Taking advantage of the establishment of large numbers of people's communes and neighborhood industrial enterprises in urban areas, urban middle and elementary schools will be able to make arrangements for their teachers and students to engage in productive labor more satisfactorily and conveniently.

Prompt reform of our school system is a very good thing for state construction and for the development of our children and youth. By carrying out exemplary experiments, the various localities have begun to find some new ways and means to achieve greater, faster, better, and more economical results in pedagogical work. This has created favorable conditions for the reform of our school system. All our education personnel should make good use of their experiences, fully develop their enthusiasm for work, actively embark on the reform program, and surmount causes for smaller, slower, poorer, and less economical results. This, I think, is what the overwhelming majority of our educational personnel will be pleased to do.

However, certain preparations must be made in carrying out any major reform program. The reform of the school system must rely on the ideological revolution as its foundation. To adhere completely to the mass line, it is necessary to carry out large-scale experiments in order to gain more experiences. It is improper to draw conclusions prematurely. Besides, conditions in different localities differ. For this reason, various provinces and municipalities should make arrangements, depending on local conditions, for conducting relatively large-scale experiments on a relatively flexible basis. On the one hand, we should fully realize the necessity and the favorable conditions for carrying out the reform of our school system, and confidently and actively carry out the reform program wherever possible and as early as possible. On the other hand, we should take the complexity of the reform program into full account, and carry it out in a prepared, systematic manner.

While carrying out the reform of middle and elementary school education, normal school education should be reformed correspondingly. An effort should be made to raise the cultural, scientific, and intellectual standards of normal colleges and normal middle schools to suitable levels equal to those of regular universities and middle schools.

All education courses should be practical and highly streamlined. An effort should be made to intensify Marxist-Leninist ideological and political education. The reform of the school system will pose greater demands on teachers. For this reason, it is necessary at the present time to raise the standards of incumbent teachers. They should be directed to master all the subjects which they will teach so that they will be able to take on their new teaching responsibilities quickly.

To further the educational policy of the Party, to pursue the educational revolution intensively, and to thoroughly reform our school system constitute a struggle between the proletarian and the bourgeois ideologies. To pursue the educational revolution and to carry out the reform of our school system intensively, it is necessary first to carry out an intensive ideological revolution, to arm ourselves with Mao Tse-tung ideology, and to thoroughly condemn the bourgeois ideology of "education for education's sake" and other erroneous viewpoints, in order to turn us into true promoters of the reform of our school system. The Ministry of Education should be the first to contribute greatly to this cause.

### III

The tasks stipulated in the national economic plan submitted by Vice Premier Li Fu-chun in his report call for the adoption of diverse measures under strengthened leadership with over-all planning to develop fully the enthusiasm of all sections in the society to develop education with greater, faster, better, and more economical results.

To develop education, we must firmly adhere to the educational policy of the Party, the policy of coordinating the work of extending universal education to all persons with the task of raising the standards of education, the policy of "walking on two legs," and the policy of actively developing higher education and middle school education, speeding up the universalization of elementary school education, and enormously developing spare-time education among the workers and peasants. Educational institutions should take the work of supporting agriculture as their glorious, important task. More schools to serve the interests of local production and construction should be established. An effort should be made to assist in the development of education in the minority nationality areas and in areas noted for their backward education.

Vice Premier Li Fu-chun has outlined the main educational targets for 1960. I have so far discussed a number of important questions in general education. Now I will elaborate on the following points with regard to the ways and means of fulfilling our tasks satisfactorily this year:

1. Actively develop full-time higher education and vocational education, and raise the standards to much higher levels. In accordance with the policy of coordinating large-scale development with over-all arrangements, we should quickly include the most advanced sciences and technology needed by our country in the

curricula of our full-time higher education institutions. In the meantime, we should pay special attention to the development of such basic sciences as mathematics, physics, chemistry, biology, and electronics, in order to lay a good foundation for the development of our sciences and technology and for raising them to higher levels.

We should rearrange our curricula, add new courses, and revise our curricular materials. Under the premise that pedagogy is to be treated as the main task, an effort should be made to strengthen scientific research, to place politics in command, to coordinate schooling with reality, to adhere closely to the mass line, to pay constant attention to the coordination of schooling with productive labor and scientific research, to develop the communist cooperative spirit, and to strengthen cooperation between educational institutions and other quarters.

Pedagogy in liberal arts colleges and scientific research in higher institutions should be further reformed to condemn the bourgeois ideology and modern revisionism, to expand and consolidate the position of Marxism-Leninism, to promote the development of philosophy and social science, and to speed up the growth of theoretical forces. Concentrated efforts should be made to establish a number of selected higher institutions to provide postgraduate departments for training large numbers of students. An active effort should be made to develop middle-school level vocational schools to train intermediate level construction personnel.

To lend great support to the development of agriculture and to speed up the training of specialized personnel for modernizing our agricultural operations, we should increase the number of students majoring in agricultural courses and strengthen the courses related to the mechanization of agricultural production. A great effort should be made to develop and properly operate agricultural middle schools to speed up the universalization of junior middle school education to benefit the development of agricultural production and the modernization of agricultural operations.

2. The universal development of spare-time educa-

tion for workers and peasants is the fundamental way to turn large numbers of workers and peasants into intellectuals in a short time. It is also one of the most important methods of training personnel for all fields of construction. According to statistics compiled in February 1960, of all workers below forty-five years of age engaged in industrial production, capital construction, transportation, communications, finance, trade, agriculture, forestry, water conservancy, and meteorological operations, more than 19 million are attending schools—more than 4.6 million are in literacy classes, more than 8.8 million are in spare-time elementary schools, more than 5 million are in spare-time middle schools, and more than 160,000 are in spare-time higher educational institutions. In the vast rural areas, more than 130 million peasants are studying in spare-time schools.

On the basis of this development, if we can first eliminate illiteracy and then universalize spare-time elementary school education and develop spare-time middle school education and higher education on a large scale, what an enormous technical force we shall possess in from three to five years! We can anticipate that by the time of the Third Five-Year Plan or a little later, we shall have millions upon millions of students in spare-time higher educational institutions and middle-school level vocational schools. This is a matter of very great significance to us.

Spare-time education should be developed according to local conditions. Night schools, correspondence schools, radio classes, and television classes should be set up wherever possible. Under conditions where production tasks are guaranteed, where the policy of "coordinating education with production, cordinating over-all arrangements, providing education for the gifted, and flexible education methods" is adhered to, we shall most assuredly be able to direct the masses to continue their study on a lasting basis, and to continually consolidate and raise the levels of our spare-time education program. Reform of the school system is also needed in spare-time schools. Due attention should be paid to this matter.

3. Actively develop child education in order to raise the next generation properly. This is also a matter of great significance to the total emancipation of our women for state economic construction and to the consolidation and development of rural and urban people's communes. To carry out child education properly, it is necessary to formulate proper plans, to develop actively the teacher training programs in child education, to open large numbers of short-term training classes for these teachers, and to step up the training of qualified teachers and nurses for nurseries.

4. Develop the operation of schools by the entire Party and the entire nation on an even larger scale. Urge all classes to develop fully their enthusiasm for this work. All factories, mines, enterprises, scientific research institutes, government organizations, people's organizations, units of the armed forces, people's communes, and urban street governments can open their own schools. They can open spare-time and part-time schools and also full-time schools; and they can operate institutions of higher education, middle-school level vocational schools, as well as regular middle schools, elementary schools, and kindergartens. These schools can formulate flexible education plans according to their specific needs.

In the course of developing education on a large scale, we should adhere to the policy of coordinating the universalization of education with the raising of our educational standards. On the one hand, we should establish as many schools as we can in an effort to universalize education and, on the other hand, we should try our best to raise the standards of selected schools to higher levels. Both the central and local authorities should perfect the operations of a number of selected schools of different categories at different levels, where particular attention is being paid to the promotion of their educational standards in order to gain experiences for wide adoption by other schools.

5. Actively participate in the nationwide technical innovation and technical revolution campaign, and introduce this campaign into schools. Recently, several

hundred thousand teachers and students of the higher education institutions and middle-school level vocational schools in the various localities have enthusiastically participated in the upsurging technical innovation and technical revolution campaign. In the course of this campaign, they have tightened their ties with workers and peasants, developed the communist spirit of thinking and acting boldly and the communist cooperative spirit, come forward with many inventions and creations, and undergone severe ideological training. In the meantime, they have also launched a campaign for the renovation of pedagogical equipment. In the spirit of relying on one's own efforts, the great masses of teachers and students coordinated their productive labor with scientific research, experimented in the production of new products, produced various apparatuses and other modern pedagogical equipment, and created and renovated other pedagogical facilities in their schools.

With the assistance of related authorities, the educational authorities at the various levels are making preparations for the construction and expansion of laboratories and scientific and educational movie and slide studies in an effort to electrify pedagogical operations.

Large-scale participation in production by schools greatly benefits the task of coordinating schools with production units and scientific research units, the development of the most advanced branches of sciences, and the task of raising the educational and scientific standards in our country. The great mass campaign of cooperation between schools and other units and between intellectuals and the masses of workers and peasants has combined the ideological, technical, and cultural revolutions into one. This is a matter of tremendous significance to the extension of the educational revolution, the reform of our school system, and the development of our education program with greater, faster, better, and more economical results.

The basic guarantee for the success of our work lies in our reliance on the leadership of the Party and in our persistence in placing politics in command. In the face of the new development and new tasks all educational personnel in our country should rely more closely on the leadership of the Party, place politics in command, diligently study Marxism-Leninism and Mao Tse-tung's works, resolutely adhere to the mass line, and actively reform pedagogical work, in order to develop our education program with greater, faster, better, and more economical results.

# 7: Education Must Be Combined with Productive Labor

## By LU TING–YI

*The author of this article is head of the Propaganda Department of the Central Committee of the Chinese Communist Party and Vice Premier of the State Council. In the former capacity, he is the highest party official in charge of formulation of educational policy. The following excerpt is taken from the English translation of this article, published in 1958 by the Foreign Languages Press, Peking.*

We are Marxists and so we maintain that it is necessary to proceed from objective reality. Therefore we must first study our own condition seriously and take to it with enthusiasm. We also study the experiences of our fraternal countries seriously, and we study history seriously, but our purpose is not to copy or transplant but to understand history, understand historical materialism in the field of education, so as to have examples for study with the aid of which we can do our work satisfactorily in accordance with our own conditions. Whatever work we do, we must rely closely on the leadership of the Party because it is none but the Communist Party that understands our conditions best and knows Marxism best. The Communist Party is the highest form of organization of the working class; it must and can give leadership in everything. From the Central Committee down to the basic organizations, the Communist Party is the organized, disciplined vanguard of the working class. We have relied on this vanguard for victory in the revolutionary war and for success in the socialist revolution on the economic, political, and ideological fronts and we must rely on it for victory in the technical and cultural revolutions. Our educational workers should accept Party leadership not only in politics but also in the sphere of educational ideas, policy, and work. Only in this way will it be possible to keep up with the times and avoid mistakes or make fewer mistakes.

In the final analysis, the debate on education that has been going on in recent years boils down to the question of "what is all-round development." Marxists believe in "producing fully developed human beings" and in achieving this through education. It is well that our educationalists often talk about all-round development. Yet there are differences of principle in the interpretation of all-round development. Judging by our country's experience in education in the past nine years, although the bourgeois pedagogues do not directly and openly oppose all-round development and even appear to "support the principle actively," yet they interpret it one-sidedly as meaning education through learning of extensive book knowledge. They do not hold with students studying politics and participating in productive labor. In fact they vulgarize the idea of all-round development and equate it with the bourgeois educational line which rears "know-alls."

We Communists interpret all-round development in an entirely different way. The essence of all-round development is that the students should acquire comparatively broader knowledge, become versatile people capable of "going over in sequence from one branch of production to another, depending on the requirements of society or their own inclinations" (F. Engels: *Principles of Communism*). We maintain that civilians should take up military service and retired military men go back to production. We maintain that cadres should participate in physical labor and productive workers in administration. All these propositions are already being put into practice gradually. Measures such as these which involve both the division of labor and change of work conform to the needs of society. They are more reasonable than the division of labor under the capitalist system. They not only increase production but enable the state to carry out reasonable readjustment of the productive forces when this becomes socially necessary, without causing social upheaval.

Our leap forward in industry and agriculture is already giving rise to the problem of the partial transfer of producers to other branches of production when what they are making grows in output to the point where it meets the current maximum demands of the people and there is even a surplus. Without such transfer there would be failure to meet the demands of the people, to develop the productive forces of society continuously and raise the people's living standards continuously. Our educational and other relevant spheres of work must prepare the ground for such transfers. Education should enable the students to acquire broad knowledge. But how broad depends on concrete objective and subjective conditions. In the future, when communist society is fully consolidated, developed and mature, men will be trained in many kinds of work and be able to undertake many professions while specializing in selected fields. This is what we aim at. We must march to this goal.

In our country's present condition, we can train people to do many kinds of work, but cannot yet train "people to be capable of undertaking any profession." The essence of all-round development is also that the knowledge imparted to the students must be not one-sided and fragmentary, but comparatively complete knowledge. This requires that education should serve politics and be combined with productive labor. Speaking of his ideal of education in the future, Karl Marx referred to "an education that will, in the case of every child over a given age, combine productive labor with instruction and gymnastics, not only as one of the methods of adding to the efficiency of production, but as the only method of producing fully developed human beings" (*Capital,* volume I). That is, he urged that students acquire comparatively complete knowledge and be able to engage not only in mental labor but manual labor as well. Book knowledge alone, however broad, is still partial and incomplete. People with extensive book knowledge alone and without experience of practical work are only what the bourgeoisie call "know-alls." They are not what we regard as people of all-round development. Physical development must be sound. In addition, a communist spirit and style and collective heroism should be inculcated in childhood. This is the moral education of our day. Both are linked with the development of intellectual education. Both are related to manual work and therefore the principle of combining education with labor is unshakable.

In brief, the all-round development we stand for is this: Students should be enabled to acquire comparatively complete, broader knowledge, grow up physically fit, and acquire communist morals. In his "On the Correct Handling of Contradictions Among the People," Comrade Mao Tse-tung said: "Our educational policy must enable everyone who gets an education to develop morally, intellectually, and physically and become a cultured, socialist-minded worker." This is our educational principle of all-round development. "A cultured, socialist-minded worker" is a man who is both politically conscious and educated. He is able to understand both mental and manual work. He is what we regard as developed in an all-round way, both politically and professionally qualified. He is a worker-intellectual and an intellectual-worker.

We insist on the educational principle of all-round development. We consider that the only method to train human beings in all-round development is to educate them to serve working-class politics and combine education with productive labor. We say the only method, because there is no other way to achieve this aim. Bourgeois pedagogues do not agree. They consider the only method to train people to have what they call "all-round development" is to read books and learn by rote. They are absolutely against students learning politics and, in particular, students becoming laborers. According to our educational principle of all-round development, we can and must rely on the masses to run education. According to the bourgeois educational principle of so-called "all-round development," they can rely only on experts to run education; they cannot rely on the masses. According to our educational principle of all-round development, education must be under the leadership of the Communist Party. According to the bourgeois educational principle of so-called "all-round development," education can only be led by experts; it does not need the leadership of the Communist Party as the Communist Party is "a layman." From this we see that different interpretations of all-round development lead to different and even opposite conclusions. That is why we say that the debate on education in recent years ultimately boils down to the question of "what is all-round development." This is essentially a struggle between proletarian and bourgeois educational ideas.

If we followed our bourgeois pedagogues' attitude toward knowledge, toward education as the business of the people, toward leadership by the Communist Party, and toward all-round development, our educational work would be dragged back to the old bourgeois road. Precisely because of this, it is necessary to give a clear explanation of our communist interpretation of these questions.

Great achievements have been made in our educational work, under the leadership of the Chinese Communist Party, in the past nine years since the founding of the People's Republic of China. These are—the recovery of the right to run education, a right formerly usurped by the imperialists; the satisfactory taking over of the schools all over the country; the abolition of the fascist system of school management practiced by the Kuomintang reactionary clique; the abolition of its fascist education and domination of the students by its special agents; the setting up of a socialist educational system; and the wiping out, in the main, of the counter-revolutionaries and other bad elements hidden in educational circles. In addition, courses in Marxism-Leninism have been opened in the schools; ideological remolding has been conducted among the teachers and students; the universities and departments have been reorganized and teaching systems reformed; and struggles have been waged against the bourgeois rightists. The number of students in institutions of higher learning, middle schools, and primary schools has in all cases increased severalfold; big advances have been made in the campaign against illiteracy and in spare-time cultural and technical education; the policy of working while studying has begun to be applied in all schools; organizations of the Chinese Communist Party have been established among the educational workers; and large numbers of people have been trained as cadres for socialist construction.

But the struggle between working-class and bourgeois ideas proceeds continuously on the educational front. This is in the nature of a struggle between the socialist and the capitalist roads. Bourgeois thinking has hampered the development of education. When the bourgeois rightists made their ferocious attacks, they even attempted to use the students as a stepping stone for the restoration of capitalism. This was at one time the dream of Chang Po-chun, Lo Lung-chi, Tseng Chao-lun, Chien Wei-chang, and others of their like. Our victory in the antirightist struggle and the great leap forward in industry and agriculture have turned bad things to good account and enabled people to understand better the danger and baneful consequences of bourgeois thinking in educational work. The work in the past nine years has given us experience and enabled us to explain our Party's policy of educational work more clearly and systematically.

The chief mistake or defect in our educational work has been the divorce of education from productive labor. The policy of combining education with productive labor was put forward by our Party early in 1934. Comrade Mao Tse-tung already then said: "What is the general policy for the Soviet[1] culture and education? It is to educate the broad masses of the toiling people in the spirit of communism, to make culture and education serve the revolutionary war and the class struggle, to combine education with labor, and to enable the broad masses of the Chinese people to enjoy civilization and happiness." In 1954 when the period of economic rehabilitation was over and the First Five-Year Plan was already in operation, the Central Committee of the Party raised the question of adding productive labor to the curricula of the schools. But the proposal encountered obstruction and was not carried through at that time. The Central Committee of the Party repeatedly stressed its policy that education must be combined with productive labor—at the national conference on propaganda work in March 1957, in the editorial of *Renmin Ribao (People's Daily)* on April 8 of the same year, and at the Nanning meeting in January 1958. It is only now that this policy of the Party has been carried out on a nationwide scale. Education must serve politics, must be combined with productive labor, and must be led by the Party—these three things are interrelated. Education divorced from productive labor is bound to lead, to a degree, to the neglect of politics and of Party leadership in educational work, thus divorcing education from the realities of our country and eventually causing right deviationist and doctrinaire mistakes.

The combination of education with productive labor is required by our country's socialist revolution and socialist construction, by the great goal of building a communist society, and by the need to develop our education with greater, faster, better, and more economical results.

The aim of our socialist revolution is to wipe out all exploiting classes, all systems of exploitation, including their remnants. Basic victory has now been won in the socialist revolution on the economic front. On the political and ideological fronts, too, the socialist revolution has achieved decisive victory. As the Second Session of

1 This refers to the Soviet areas in China which existed at that time under the leadership of the Chinese Communist Party.

the Eighth National Congress of the Communist Party of China has pointed out in its resolution, our task is "to carry out actively the technical and cultural revolutions while continuing with the socialist revolution on the economic, political, and ideological fronts."

The cultural revolution is to enable all 600 million Chinese people, except for those who are incapable, to do productive work and to study. This means to make the masses of our workers and peasants intellectuals as well and our intellectuals laborers too. Only when the masses of the workers and peasants and the intellectuals alike develop along the line of making up what they lack is it possible to change thoroughly the irrational legacy of the old society and eradicate the backwardness of each, i.e., eliminate the cultural deficiency of the masses of workers and peasants and eliminate the bourgeois thinking of the intellectuals. This is, therefore, a very far-reaching revolution which demands that education must serve working-class politics, that is be combined with productive labor.

Marx said: "An early combination of productive labor with education is one of the most potent means for the transformation of present-day society" (Karl Marx: *Critique of the Gotha Programme*). It is impossible to carry through the cultural revolution without combining education with productive labor. Cultural revolution is beneficial to the country, to the masses of workers and peasants as well as to the intellectuals. Only those who stick to the bourgeois standpoint do not want such a revolution. The bourgeois policy of education for education's sake, and divorcing mental from physical labor, is incompatible with the socialist revolution.

Our socialist construction demands the utmost effort and consistent pressing ahead; it demands building the country industriously and thriftily; it also demands technique and culture and the training of large numbers of socialist-minded and professionally proficient technicians in conformity with the principle of achieving greater, faster, better, and more economical results. These needs of socialist construction also demand the combination of education with productive labor. Lenin said: "It is impossible to visualize the ideal of future society without combining the training and education of the young generation with productive labor. Neither training and education without productive labor, nor productive labor without parallel training and education could have been raised to the height demanded by present-day technique and the state of scientific knowledge" (Pearls of Narodniks' Hare-brained Schemes). The policy of combining education with productive labor will certainly raise the quality of education. This holds true for intellectual and for moral and physical education. The educational policy of divorcing mental and manual labor cannot meet the needs of socialist construction.

The future communist society will be one of "from each according to his ability and to each according to his needs," a society in which the differences between town and country and between mental and manual labor are eliminated. Our big leap forward in industry and agriculture has made the attainment of communism no longer a far distant prospect. One hundred and ten years ago Marx and Engels in the *Communist Manifesto* formulated ten measures to establish a communist society, which "will be pretty generally applicable . . . in the most advanced countries." Of these, the first eight have already been carried out in China, through the adoption of methods suitable to the actual conditions of our country; and the last two, namely "the combination of agriculture with manufacturing industries; the gradual abolition of the distinction between town and country" and "the combination of education with industrial production," are beginning to be carried out.

It is clear to everyone that because of the application, in the course of industrial development, of the policy "to develop industry and agriculture simultaneously while giving priority to heavy industry; and, with centralized leadership, over-all planning, proper division of labor, and coordination to develop national and local industries, and large, small, and medium-sized enterprises simultaneously," industry has appeared in the rural areas and, with it, the phenomenon of workers who are simultaneously peasants and peasants who are simultaneously workers. This phenomenon has the embryo of communist society.

Because the principle of combining education with productive labor is beginning to go into operation, with schools setting up their own factories and farms, and factories and agricultural cooperatives establishing their own schools on a large scale, the phenomenon of students who are at the same time workers and peasants and of workers and peasants who are students at the same time is beginning to appear. This, too, has the embryo of communist society. It can be imagined that when China enters into communism, our basic social organizations will be many communist communes. With few exceptions, each basic unit will have workers, peasants, traders, students, and militia. In the field of education, each basic unit will have its own primary and secondary schools and institutions of higher learning; at the same time everybody will have the time to acquire education as both laborer and intellectual. In *The Housing Question* Engels anticipated this situation when he said: "And it is precisely this industrial revolution which has raised the productive power of human labor among all, of producing not only enough for the plentiful consumption of all members of society and for an abundant reserve fund, but also of leaving each individual sufficient leisure so that what is really worth preserving in historically inherited culture—science, art, forms of intercourse—may not only be preserved but converted from a monopoly of the ruling class into the common property of the whole of society, and may be further developed." To attain this prospect, our educational work must not go in the direction of divorcing mental and manual labor but in the direction of combining mental with manual labor and education with productive labor.

To the bourgeois educationalists it seems impossible to get greater, faster, better, and more economical results in education. But the tremendous growth in educational work can make it develop with greater, faster, better, and more economical results. The combination of education with labor, making education an activity that is warmly welcomed by the workers and peasants, is an important way of arousing mass initiative in the setting up of schools. The principles of running schools by applying the mass line under Communist Party leadership are: First, to combine unity with diversity. The purpose of the training is unified, that is, to train socialist-minded, educated workers; but the schools can be run by the central or local authorities, factories and mines, enterprises and agricultural cooperatives, and the forms the schools can take are varied. They may be full-time, or part-work part-study, or spare-time schools; they may collect fees or be free of charge. As production grows further and working hours can be shortened, the present spare-time schools will be similar to part-work part-study schools. When production develops considerably and public accumulation rises greatly, the schools that now charge fees will similarly become free.

Second, to combine the spreading of education widely with the raising of educational levels. The level of education must be raised on the basis of popularization and popularization must be so guided as to raise the level of education. Some of the full-time, the part-work part-study, and the spare-time schools undertake the task of raising educational levels at the same time as education is being spread extensively through part-work part-study and spare-time courses. Since the schools that popularize education are part-work part-study or spare-time schools, they can meet the whole or the greater part of their expenditures themselves, and can find teachers locally in accordance with the principle that "every capable person can teach." They can develop gradually by perfecting their curricula, equipment and teaching staff with aid from the government. In schools where courses in labor are lacking, the stress should be on introducing them, and in schools where the deficiency is in the basic courses the stress should be on introducing these, so that both kinds of schools go forward to fill in what they lack and apply the principle of combining theory with practice more effectively.

Third, to combine over-all planning with decentralization, to bring into play the initiative of both the various central government departments and the local authorities, guided by the Party committees, to develop education as fast as possible and enable this development to benefit, not hamper, the growth of production.

Fourth, to apply the mass line in the political, administrative, pedagogic, and research work in the schools. In all such work, it is necessary, guided by the Party committees, to adopt the method of open and free airing of views, and *tatsepao* and the method of the "three combinations" (for instance, in working out teaching plans and programs, the method can be adopted of combining the efforts of the teachers and the students under the leadership of the Party committee, and so on), and to establish democratic relations of equality—changing the old irrational relations—between the teachers and the students. Experience shows that remarkable achievements have been made where these methods have been adopted.

A struggle has to be waged before the combination of education with labor is effected, and this struggle will be a protracted one. Why? Because this is a revolution upsetting old traditions in educational work that have persisted for thousands of years. The principle of divorcing mental from manual labor has dominated educational work for thousands of years. All the exploiting classes in history have adhered firmly to this principle. More than two thousand years ago, Confucius took a stand against combining education with productive labor. He condemned Fan Chih[2] who "requested to be

2 The *Analects* record a conversation between Fan Chih, disciple of Confucius, and Confucius. Fan Chih said that he wanted to learn farming; Confucius said that he was not so good a teacher as the peasant. Fan Chih said that he wanted to learn how to plant vegetables; Confucius said that he was not so good a teacher as the kitchen-garden keeper. After Fan Chih had left Confucius told his other disciples that Fan Chih was a man with no great ambition. This conversation shows that Confucius had a contempt for productive labor and that he was against the combination of education with production.

taught husbandry" and "requested to be taught garden-ing" as a "small man." Mencius opposed Hsu Hsing,[3] saying: "Those who labor with their minds govern oth-ers; those who labor with their strength are governed by others. Those who are governed by others support them; those who govern others are supported by them. This is a principle universally recognized." On this point, bourgeois pedagogues are in full accord with Confucius and Mencius. Originally, education was linked with pro-ductive labor, but was separated in class society: now the link will be reforged.

Fourier and Owen, the Utopian socialists of the eight-eenth century, were the first to put forward the idea of combining education with productive labor. Marx, En-gels, and Lenin all endorsed this idea. In volume I of *Capital* Marx expressed the view that a part-work part-study system of schooling was more suitable for children than full-time study. In "The Directive to the Delegates of the Provisional Central Council on Some Questions" he suggested: "In a reasonable social order every child must become a productive worker starting at the age of nine."

He maintained that children from the age of nine to twelve should do two hours' work every day in a work-shop or at home, children from thirteen to fifteen years of age four hours, and from sixteen to seventeen years of age six hours. He believed that "the combination of re-munerative productive labor, mental education, physical exercise, and polytechnical training elevates the working class considerably above the level of the higher and mid-dle classes." Marx once foretold that "there can be no doubt that when the working class comes into power, as inevitably it must, technical instruction, both theoretical

3 Hsu Hsing, a thinker of the Warring States period, held the theory that all men, be they kings or common people, should till the land and weave cloth themselves. Mencius did not agree with Hsu Hsing. He held that those who work with their brain govern while those who engage in manual labor are governed. Those who are governed must support those who govern. From this we can see that Mencius was against the combination of brain work and manual labor.

and practical, will take its proper place in the working-class schools" (*Capital,* volume I). Only in a socialist country led by the working class and the Communist Party can the principle of combining education with productive labor be carried into effect and play a great role in revolution and construction. Marx's prophecy will come true in our country.

We must realize that to carry the combination of education with productive labor into effect means a fight with the old traditions that have persisted for thousands of years. Without the communist style of toppling down the old idols, burying doctrinairism, and daring to think, speak, and do, without the creative spirit of combining the universal truths of Marxism with the concrete realities of our country, we cannot succeed. Today, in our educational work, vigorous efforts are being made to pull down the outdated and set up the new. Bourgeois and doctrinaire ideas are being broken down and new, Marxist educational theories, systems and methods, curricula and school systems suited to our country are being created. This educational revolution has solid economic foundations. The Marxist doctrine of historical materialism teaches that the superstructure must conform to the economic base. The political system is superstructure, the concentrated expression of economic life. Education comes into the category of ideology and is also superstructure; it serves politics. Class society which has existed for thousands of years has had ownership by slave-owners, landlords, or capitalists as its economic base. The political systems that conform to these types of education that serve these dictatorships are those of the slave-owners, the landlords, and the bourgeoisie. These types of education differ from each other, but all have this in common, that education is divorced from productive labor, mental from manual labor, and manual labor and laborers are despised. The divorce of mental from manual labor is needed by all the exploiting classes, including the bourgeoisie.

Our society has socialist ownership as its economic base. The political system suited to socialist ownership is proletarian dictatorship. Our education serves the proletarian dictatorship. Therefore, contrary to the old traditions that persisted for thousands of years, it must apply the principle of combining education with productive labor so as to eliminate the difference between mental and manual labor; and this also means wiping out the survivals of all the systems of exploitation that have existed in history, so that humanity may enter into communist society.

The principle of combining education with productive labor is needed by the working class and all other working people. This principle, which conforms to the people's desires, will certainly prevail. On the other hand, the principle of divorcing mental from manual labor, since it does not conform to the socialist economic base and the people's requirements, will sooner or later be discarded by the people even though it has a tradition of thousands of years. With politics in command, with leadership by the Communist Party, and with the rallying of the entire Party and all educational workers who can be rallied to fight against bourgeois educational policy and for the application of the Party's educational policy, we can so carry through our cultural revolution that all of our 600 million people are able to do productive work and all are able to study, changing them into new men who are both laborers and intellectuals.

# 8: Our Schooling System Must Be Reformed

## By LU TING–YI

*This speech by Lu Ting-yi, chief of the Propaganda De-
partment of the Central Committee of the Chinese Communist Party and concurrently Vice Premier of the State
Council, was delivered at the Second Session of the Second National People's Congress, April 1960. The long-
range plan for school reform in China is spelled out in
this document which is available in English in* Current
Background *(No. 623, U.S. Consulate General, Hong
Kong).*

We plan, beginning now, to carry out a large-scale experimentation on reducing the number of years spent in
education, raising the standards, controlling the study
hours, and increasing physical labor to a suitable extent
in our full-time middle and elementary schools.

We plan to carry out a reform program on the schooling system step by step and phase by phase in our full-
time middle and elementary schools in the next ten to
twenty years.

To carry out the education of our people properly will
require a prolonged trial-and-error process. We must ac-
cumulate experiences in this work. Marxism-Leninism
and the Mao Tse-tung ideology are our guiding ideologies; this is clear to all of us. However, the question of

their application to educational work cannot be solved all at once.

In the past eleven years, our education work has achieved tremendous progress. Since 1958 when the Chinese Communist Party Central Committee and the State Council issued a directive on educational revolution, we have rapidly developed our education. We have markedly changed and raised to higher levels our schooling standards with regard to the moral, academic, and physical cultural standards of our students.

We can now adopt this goal in our struggle: A great effort must be made to complete in the main the elimination of illiteracy among our young and adult workers and peasants, and to provide universal elementary school education to all school-age children in the period of the Second Five-Year Plan. A great effort must also be made, through the adoption of the policy of "walking on two legs," to provide junior middle school education to all the youths of appropriate age; greatly develop senior middle schools, vocational schools, and higher education institutions; establish a number of short-term college-level vocational schools, develop spare-time educational institutions of all categories, and train for the state a great force of "red-and-expert" scientific and technological personnel and Marxist-Leninist theorists in the period of the Third Five-Year Plan.

The fulfillment of these tasks will entail an enormous effort, and nothing short of this will do. Even then, the development of education will be unable to satisfy the needs of the various quarters for socialist construction. Where, then, does the problem lie? The problem lies in the fact that our school system has been carried out with smaller, slower, poorer, and less economical results. For this reason, we must carry out a reform in our schooling system.

Our present schooling system was inherited from the Kuomintang rule—a backward schooling system copied from the United States. It is characterized by a great number of years spent in elementary and middle schools, making it hard to extend school education to all and to raise school education to higher levels.

The long schooling period and the low school standards are detrimental to state construction, to the progress of the students, and to the interests of our future generations. We have carried out a degree of educational reform in the past with some success. We have not yet, however, had a chance to embark on the reform of our middle and elementary schools.

The bourgeois educational system is, of course, a step forward from the landlord-class education system. Otherwise, our country would not have abolished our native schooling system in favor of a modern schooling system. But bourgeois education aims at a much lower goal than does working-class education. Moreover, the bourgeois education system has a reactionary aspect. The bourgeois education system aims at the extension of so-called "compulsory education" to all the people.

What is "compulsory education"? According to this system, the laboring people are, on the one hand, coerced into receiving some education, while, on the other hand, they are prevented from receiving higher education. Thus they will have enough knowledge to run the machines of the capitalists without wrecking them, and yet not enough education to place themselves academically on a par with the intellectuals of the bourgeoisie. Under this system, only the wealthy, who do not have to worry about their livelihood even though they do not engage in labor, have the opportunity to receive higher education and to become bourgeois intellectuals and advance the interests of the bourgeoisie and rule the laboring people.

The goal of our educational system is entirely different from that of the bourgeois system. We want to extend education of high standards to all our people, and to raise our communist consciousness and moral standards to much higher levels, in order to eliminate the difference between mental and manual labor. This goal is, of course, much greater and more glorious than that of the "compulsory education" system.

Differences in social class and in goal call for the adoption of different policies and methods. We hold that education should be directed to serve the political interests of the proletariat. The bourgeois slogan of "education for education's sake" identifies the bourgeois educational system as one for advancing the political interests of the bourgeoisie. While we hold that education should be co-ordinated with productive labor, the bourgeoisie hold that education should be separated from productive labor. While we hold that education should be led by the Party and be carried out according to the mass line, the bourgeoisie hold that schools must be directed by experts, and be carried out according to the "expert" line.

Furthermore, our stand for rapidly developing education according to the policy of "walking on two legs" is different from that of the bourgeoisie, which would restrict the development of education.

There are also two stands on the schooling system: While we hold that schools should be run with greater, faster, better, and more economical results, bourgeois scholars are satisfied with the smaller, slower, poorer, and less economical results brought about through their own schooling system. It is to the advantage of the bourgeoisie and not of the working class to have a longer schooling period and lower standards for middle and elementary schools.

The bourgeois theory of education adheres to the principle of "to each according to his ability." This principle has a correct side—not to let students shoulder too heavy burdens but to educate the students according to their talents—and this same principle should be applied in our educational system. However, the principle of "to each according to his ability" of the bourgeois educational theory is one designed to defend the smaller, slower, poorer, and less economical results in the bourgeois educational system, and to make it hard for the laboring people to receive higher education.

This can clearly be understood in the following instances which occurred in our country: At the time when the Kuomintang extended the period of elementary and middle school education from the previous eleven years to twelve years, the bourgeois educators did not say that it was inconsistent with the principle of "to each according to his ability." Since the liberation of our country, although much progress has been made in middle and elementary school education in general, the cultural standards have been lowered in some respects as exemplified by the elimination of analytical geometry from the curricula of senior middle schools and the adoption of lower standards in foreign languages. These measures for lowering the standards of education did not, however, raise the opposition of the bourgeois educators, and nobody has said that these measures are at variance with the principle of "to each according to his ability."

Now, just as we advance the theory that our schooling system should be designed to bring about greater, faster, better, and more economical results, the principle of "to each according to his ability" is played up as a theoretical weapon against the reform of our schooling system. However, the fact that middle and elementary schools are being operated with smaller, slower, poorer, and less economical results is so plain that it is impossible for anyone to speak in its defense. We fully believe that an overwhelming majority—more than 90 per cent—of those in education circles are in favor of the reform of our schooling system, that only a very small number of people are opposed to this reform. Those who would intimidate us with the bourgeois theory of education will decidedly meet with frustration.

Since 1958, educational reform personnel in our country have carried out experiments on the reform of the schooling system, of the curricula of middle and elementary schools, and of teaching methods in the various localities. Although it has not been very long since these experiments were carried out, it can now be seen that the reform of our schooling system is a realistic project, not a dream. I would like now to cite a few instances with regard to the experiments:

1. The present schooling system stipulates that pupils in kindergartens should not be taught reading and arithmetic. However, experiments carried out in Hopei,

Shansi, Liaoning, Heilungkiang, Shensi, Kansu, Tsinghai, Shanghai, Kiangsu, Shantung, Fukien, Hupeh, and Honan show that even large kindergarten classes are able to learn how to spell Chinese words with the alphabet and to learn to read from 80 to 100 Chinese words. Experiments carried out in Heilungkiang, Kansu, Kiangsu, Honan, and Liaoning show that large kindergarten classes are able to calculate figures up to 20. The adoption of the methods of learning through playing is not only harmless to the health of the children concerned, but also makes the kindergartens more attractive to the children and their parents.

2. The prevailing schooling system stipulates that only children who have reached the age of seven can be admitted. But experiments in Peking, Kirin, Kansu, and many other localities show that it is practicable to admit children of six. It seems that it is practicable to admit children of six, six and a half, and seven years of age into schools according to the development of the child concerned.

3. Beginning in September 1958, with the assistance of a work team of the Psychology Research Institute of the Chinese Academy of Sciences, the Chinese Communist Party committee of Heishan *hsien* in Liaoning carried out an experiment on language study with the method of "collective study and collective exercise" at Peikuan Elementary School in the *hsien*. In five weeks, the committee completed the first volume of the language textbook published by the Education Ministry of the Central People's Government—containing 233 new words —for teaching pupils of the first grade. By the end of the first semester, the committee had taught the pupils 1,700 words, with each pupil mastering an average of 1,115 words—with the best pupils mastering all 1,700 words, and the worst mastering 400. This shows that in one semester pupils of the first grade may progress to the level of the second grade stipulated by the Education Ministry. (The first four volumes of the language textbook published by the Education Ministry contain 1,230 new words.)

In addition, the pupils are able to write short essays and to keep diaries. This experimental class has now progressed to the second grade. On January 10 of this year, Deputy Governor Che Hsiang-chen paid a visit to that school. Liu Yin, a pupil in this experimental class, wrote a poem in his honor: "Uncle Che is a busy man, yet he has time to see us in person. He listens to a lecture and takes some pictures. We shall never forget him." Please note that this is a poem written by a pupil in the second grade.

Beginning in October 1959 the Peikuan Elementary School in Heishan *hsien* in Liaoning adopted an improved method of teaching arithmetic to two classes in the second grade and two classes in the first grade on an experimental basis, and completed teaching in one month a course scheduled for a whole semester. From this it can be seen that there is plenty of room to improve our teaching system and our textbooks.

4. The Psychology Research Institute of the Chinese Academy of Sciences carried out an experiment in teaching arithmetic in coordination with algebra in two classes of the fifth grade in the No. 2 experimental elementary school in Peking with good results. At a unified examination in arithmetic held among all elementary schools in Hsicheng *ch'u,* Peking, the grades of the pupils in these two classes averaged better than 94.

The institute holds that by teaching arithmetic in coordination with algebra, some of the curricular materials for middle schools may be introduced to elementary schools in line with the reform of our schooling system. By mastering algebra, a student will be able to solve difficult problems in arithmetic very easily.

5. Fifteen provinces and municipalities—Hopei, Shansi, Liaoning, Kirin, Heilungkiang, Shensi, Kansu, Tsinghai, Shanghai, Kiangsu, Anhwei, Kiang, Hupeh, Honan, and Kweichow—are experimenting on the five-grade unified elementary school system. Because many localities have extended elementary school education to all school-age children and have combined their junior and senior elementary school education; and also because

the curricular materials of elementary schools are too re-
petitious (in the case of arithmetic, for instance, the cal-
culating method is repeated 7 times, covering figures below 10, then those below 100, then those below 1,000,
then those below 10,000, then those below 100 million,
and finally round figures), making it an easy matter to
streamline these materials, comrades in charge of education in many localities hold that it should not be difficult
to adopt the five-grade unified elementary school system. [Present elementary schools in Communist China
have six grades in the senior elementary school.]

6. Six provinces—Kirin, Shensi, Kansu, Kiangsi, Honan, and Tsinghai—are experimenting on the five-grade
unified middle school system or the three-year junior
middle school and two-year senior middle school system.
[The prevailing system is three years each for junior and
senior middle schools.]

7. Peking and Honan are experimenting on the ten-
year unified elementary and middle school systems.

There are experiments in many other categories which
I will not enumerate here. A relatively long time will be
needed to carry out the reform of our school system on
an experimental basis. We should not try to draw final
conclusions prematurely. However, it can definitely be
said that if only we can properly reform our teaching
methods, revise our textbooks, strengthen the leadership
of the Chinese Communist Party committees attached to
schools and organize large-scale coordinated cooperation
between teachers to change their present practice of each
tending his own business without coordination, it will be
quite possible for us to shorten suitably the number of
schooling years, raise the education standards, tighten
control over study hours, and increase physical labor. It
is very important to organize large-scale coordinated cooperation between teachers under the leadership of the
Chinese Communist Party committees concerned.

The main courses in full-time middle and elementary
schools are languages and mathematics. These courses
are the most fundamental tools to be mastered by students. If languages and mathematics are properly mas-

tered, it becomes relatively easy to master physics, chemistry, biology, history, and geography. The joint efforts of all teachers are needed in enabling the students to master languages and mathematics properly. On the other hand, language and mathematics teachers also have the duty to assist the students in properly mastering physics, chemistry, biology, history, geography, and other courses. By cooperating in a coordinated manner under the leadership of the Party, one-half the effort will yield twice the results. On the other hand, by practicing individualism without cooperation, twice as much effort will yield only half the result.

On the basis of their research work and experiences gained in actual practice since 1958, teachers and students of Peking Normal College advanced a nine-year unified full-time middle and elementary school system and submitted a plan for radically changing the teaching method for mathematics. This draft plan was discussed at the Chinese Mathematics Institute. All mathematicians attending the discussion voiced support for the principles contained in the draft plan. It is hoped that the Chinese Mathematics Institute will cooperate with Peking Normal College in continuing research work on this plan so that it will be perfected.

In drafting this plan, Peking Normal College has turned itself into an education-revolution university. This is a very good development. We hope that all the normal universities and colleges in China will become education-revolution universities and colleges. We hope that all the scientific, engineering, agricultural, and medical colleges will become technical-revolution colleges. We also hope that all liberal arts colleges will become revolution colleges in their own fields of study, so that they will condemn the bourgeois academic ideology and develop the Marxist-Leninist academic ideology.

The various provinces and municipalities in our country are now making concrete arrangements for carrying out large-scale experiments on their school systems according to their actual conditions. Although these are still experiments, they are being carried out on an even larger scale than before. It is believed that in the course of the experiments, more inventions and creations will be advanced to bring about greater, faster, better, and more economical results in school education.

Education and school work should be coordinated with productive labor. Participation in labor of school teachers and students aims mainly at reforming their ideology, changing the situation where education is separated from productive labor and education is alienated from reality, and improving the relationship between intellectuals on the one hand and workers and peasants on the other. This is a major political and ideological task which we must resolutely carry out.

In the past, students in rural areas could easily participate in productive labor, while those in urban areas could not do so as easily. Now, thanks to the development of urban commune-operated industry, neighborhood industry, suburban agriculture, and collective welfare undertakings, it has become easier for middle and elementary school students in urban areas to participate in productive labor.

In carrying out the reform of our school system, it is possible not only to reduce suitably the number of school years and to increase suitably educational standards, but also to tighten suitably control over study hours and to increase suitably physical labor. By suitably tightening study hours and suitably increasing physical labor, the students will be guaranteed their health, and the practice of education through labor will be strengthened. This highlights the importance of this work.

It is our preliminary intention with regard to the new school system to reduce the number of years of full-time middle and elementary school education to approximately ten, and to raise the standards of the graduates to that of freshmen of our present colleges. Why do we advocate "approximately ten years"? Because it takes approximately ten years for children who start schooling at six or seven years of age to grow to the age of sixteen or seventeen, when they will be considered as full manpower units. It is relatively easy to provide ten years' full-

time education to our children after we have completed
in the main our agricultural capital construction program
and have mechanized our agricultural production operations, inasmuch as such an educational program takes
away little or no full manpower units from production.

It is practical to adopt the ten-year unified middle and
elementary school education system and to raise the
standards of the graduates to that of freshmen of our
present colleges. If we are able to fulfill this preliminary
plan and extend ten years of school education to all of
our children in the future, all our youth will have received approximately ten years of education by the age
of sixteen or seventeen when they become full manpower
units, and all of them will have reached the educational
level of that of freshmen of our present colleges.

All students in our present senior middle schools now
are full manpower units. For this reason, we cannot
afford to extend our present senior middle school education to too many persons. We are graduating only
several hundred thousand students from senior middle
schools each year. Even if greater efforts are exerted in
this work, the best we can do will be to graduate a little
over one million students from senior middle schools each
year. Should we try to increase this number, we would
take away too much manpower from production.

On the other hand, if we put the new school system in
our mind into practice, we shall be able to graduate more
than 10 million senior middle school students a year,
without taking too much manpower away from production. This can be done because we have annually more
than 10 million youth attaining the age of sixteen or
seventeen.

With the supply of such a huge number of young senior middle school graduates who are of high educational
standards, we shall be able to direct each of our more
than 1,700 counties to establish one or more full-time
and part-time higher educational institutions, and to direct all factories, mines, enterprises, government organizations, and people's communes to open some spare-time

higher educational institutions, in addition to the higher educational institutions established by the Central People's Government, and the provincial, municipal, and special administrative area authorities. In this way, we shall be able to let all our youth above sixteen and seventeen years of age receive higher education by adhering to the policy of "walking on two legs." This highlights the spectacular development of our educational program in the future. By that time, our needs for technical and theoretical cadres will be better satisfied, our technical innovation and technical revolution campaign will develop at an increasingly high speed, and the difference between mental and manual labor will be reduced to the minimum.

This will be beneficial to the state as well as to the individuals concerned. This plan is within the capacity of our efforts and its advantage is so obvious. In the interests of the great majority of our people and of our society as a whole, we must walk this road.

It goes without saying, of course, that it is not enough to have more experiments in the reform of our school system. We must make material and ideological preparations.

1. We must raise the standards of our teachers. This calls for a reform of our normal college education and greater attention to the organization of our existing teachers colleges for advanced studies.

2. An effort should be made to place our present "double section" schools [possibly meaning senior and junior sections of present middle and elementary schools] on a full-time basis, group by group and phase by phase. After this, dormitories should be provided for all students. This requires more capital constrวtion.

3. We should operate kindergartens properly and, for this purpose, operate nurseries properly. To do so, we must greatly develop normal schools for training teachers for kindergartens and schools for training nurses for nurseries.

4. We should adopt large quantities of new educational equipment such as records, tape recorders, lantern

slides, motion pictures, radios, television, and other necessary apparatus and models.

5. Sufficient quantities of stationery should be
supplied.

All the above are needed to complete material
preparations.

With respect to ideological preparations, what we
should primarily do is thoroughly condemn bourgeois
pedagogy and develop communist educational theories.
We should combat the servile attitude toward bourgeois
pedagogy and promote the elimination of superstition,
the emancipation of minds, the spirit of thinking, speaking, and acting boldly, the full mobilization of the
masses, and the communist spirit of carrying out all programs by experiment. All our pedagogy and psychology
research institutes and normal colleges and universities
should dutifully carry out this task.

Our educational personnel should bear in mind the
interests of the society of the next generations, and of
communism, and not merely the interests of themselves
and their own profession. They should carry out large-
scale coordinated cooperation under the leadership of
the Chinese Communist Party committees concerned,
and not try to rely on their own isolated efforts.

During the periods of the rule of the Peiyang warlords
and the Kuomintang, educational personnel led a very
precarious life. As a result, they were obliged to pay
more attention to their own interests, and the practice
of individualism and egoism was prevalent at that time.
Although in the old society a small number of persons in
educational circles made some effort to carry out their
educational work faster and more properly, because they
did not have the leadership of the Communist Party, nor
the support of the reactionary government, their efforts
failed to achieve any success.

The present situation is entirely different. In the same
way as personnel in other fields, educational personnel
can completely develop their initiative. Under the leadership of the Party, educational work is growing day
after day. For this reason, our educational personnel can

afford to pay attention only to the interests of the society, the great majority of our people, the next generations, and communism in carrying out the reform of the
schooling system, without having to worry about themselves. On the other hand, the Party and the state should
take care of the personal interests of educational personnel by ensuring their livelihood, organizing them to advance their studies so that they will work more competently, maintaining their salaries at levels not lower than
their old ones in case of the transfer of their work, gradually increasing their collective welfare facilities according to government regulations, promoting their positions
regularly, and awarding them longevity bonuses in service. Educational personnel who have lost their working
ability because of their old age should be given collective
welfare benefits, so that they may lead a happy life
afterwards.

Teaching is a complex mental labor which requires
hard work. For this reason, teachers should receive due
respect. In the course of achieving tremendous forward
leaps in educational work, teachers are very busy. The
leadership should pay attention to the policy of coordinating labor with rest, and ensure that the teachers will
have sufficient time for preparing their courses, correcting the work of students, advancing their studies, and
rest.

After undergoing ideological reform and after receiving large numbers of new members, our educational personnel have greatly changed their ideological stand and
have made much progress. Large numbers of advanced
educational personnel have developed sky-rocketing work
enthusiasm and a high morale. However, it can be understood that a small number of educational personnel
may have failed to change themselves completely from
the old habit of paying attention only to their private
interests to the spirit of bearing in mind only the interests of the society, and from their bourgeois education
ideology. These personnel are in need of some sympa-
thetic and personal assistance for achieving the change.

This is a glorious task to be carried out by the advanced elements in educational circles.

We are walking a road never before traversed by our predecessors. We should walk this road with great courage, because we firmly believe it is a correct road. However, in spite of our certainty of the success of our program, inasmuch as we are carrying out experiments, we may experience partial and temporary setbacks and even partial failures. For this reason, we must not carry out any task in a reckless manner.

We stand for the necessity of discussion and experimentation in all new tasks. We hold that we should spend from ten to twenty years on the reform of the middle and elementary school educational system, phase by phase and stage by stage, without trying to achieve success in a hurry. In other words, we hold that we must not carry out our work impetuously. At the beginning, all new things are bound to develop some shortcomings. Although the shortcomings must be corrected, we should not give way to letting the shortcomings of one finger cover up the benefits of the other nine fingers.

We have now determined to walk this road. We must carry out the reform of our schooling system; we must not refrain from doing this. If we should experience any frustration and shortcoming in the course of experimentation, we should take the lesson and improve our work accordingly, without playing up such frustrations and shortcomings. If this point is agreed by all, we should adopt it as our fixed policy.

Since the educational revolution, our educational program has assumed a new, thriving look. The present schooling system reform program is a continuation of the educational revolution. It still constitutes a class struggle, including the struggle between the advanced and the backward and between the right and the wrong. Although the struggle is unavoidable, we are sure of our victory. All persons who have the great ambition of realizing communism and of developing our educational program should be united. We are determined to change the "poverty-stricken and bleak" appearance of our country, and to surpass Britain in production and all capitalist countries in education.

We fully believe that after experimentation, a new schooling system, a new pedagogical system, and new textbooks will emerge in a coordinated manner from actual practice, and new pedagogical and psychological theories will be derived therefrom.

We are not now in a hurry to issue decrees governing the new schooling system to be adopted throughout our country. Even in the future when the new schooling system is adopted, a period will be granted for the people to implement it on a trial basis. In the same way as other things, education and schooling are subject to continuous revolution. It can be foreseen that in the next scores of years or in the next century, some of the scientific knowledge which seems to be so high as to be beyond the reach of most people may become the common sense of the common people.

By that time, some change must take place in education. There is no end in the development of social production capacity, in the advancement of sciences, and in the progress of the educational ideology. For this reason, new experiments must continue to be carried out even in the far future for continually reforming our schooling system to meet the needs of the development of social production capacity, and to eliminate the difference between mental and manual labor.

# 9: Educational Revolution and Progress: 1949–1959[1]

## By YANG HSIU-FENG

*With the permission of the magazine* School and Society, *this article is reproduced here to show the way in which educational progress is presented by the Minister of Education during the first decade of Communist rule in China. Translated by Miss Lily Tsien, the article appeared in* School and Society, *volume 89, number 2198, November 4, 1961.*

Under the leadership of the Chinese Communist Party and Chairman Mao Tse-tung, education has made great strides during the past 10 years. . . .

In terms of enrollment, the figures for 1958 compared with those of 1949 are as follows: pre-schools: 31,000,000, or an increase of 237 times; elementary schools: 86,000,-000, or an increase of 2.6 times, 85% of all children of school age are now in school; secondary schools: 10,-520,000, or an increase of 5.6 times; secondary vocational schools: 1,470,000, or an increase of 2.8 times; higher education institutions: 660,000, or an increase of 3.2 times.

1 Report issued to commemorate the 10th anniversary of the People's Republic of China, printed in "Chien Kuo Shih Nien" ("Ten Years National Construction" (Hong Kong: Chi Wen Publishing, 1959), vol. 2, pp. 85–102.

During the past ten years, nearly 2,000,000 specialized personnel of higher and middle levels have been trained and nearly 100,000,000 young workers and farmers have become literate. . . .

1958 was the year of the Big Leap Forward; school enrollment drastically increased at all levels . . . including 60,000,000 attending classes for the eradication of illiteracy and over 30,000,000 in spare-time schools. . . . Since the founding of the People's Republic, steady efforts have been made to provide educational opportunities for the proletariat; by 1958, 90% of pre-school and elementary pupils were of worker-farmer origin; they constituted 70% of all secondary school students and 48% of students in higher education institutions. Among the entering students of 1958, the last ratio has increased to 62%.

When the Government of the People's Republic of China was established in 1949, we took over the schools in the nation. We eliminated in them the reactionary Kuomintang method of fascist and Gestapo control and recovered the educational establishments from the hands of the imperialists. Political education based on Marxism-Leninism was instituted; so was thought reform among teachers and students. . . . In 1957 a rectification campaign was launched to combat the rightist capitalist classes. At the same time, continuing the educational tradition developed in the former Revolutionary base[2] and learning from the advanced experience in educational matters of the Soviet Union, we brought about a systematic educational reform in accordance with socialist principles. In the higher education institutions, departments and schools were reorganized with emphasis on specialized professional training; as a result, the ratio of students in engineering and teacher training has greatly increased. (Engineering students now consist of 37% of all university students compared to 17.8% in 1949; higher normal students have increased to 24% from 13.5% in 1949.) In order to train specialized personnel for national

2 TRANSLATOR'S NOTE: This refers to Communist rule in the Shensi-Ningsha-Kansa area prior to their control of all Mainland China.

construction, over 300 specialized fields have been introduced in both higher education institutions and professional schools at the secondary levels. . . . The development of schools of various levels and types has been carried out along the lines of national planning and systematic management, while consideration is given to local characteristics and conditions. Emphasis has been given to industrial and mining areas in the interior, [and to] elementary and secondary education in agricultural villages and among minority groups. . . . Efforts have been made to group, reform, and educate teachers already in service, while new teachers are being trained. Particular mention should be made of the specialist teachers (now numbering 2,500,000 compared to 930,000 in 1949), among whom, because of their ever-increasing political consciousness and professional competence, are a vast number of model teachers and advanced workers in the struggle for educational renewal.

In 1958, our people, building on the victory attained in the economic, political, and ideological fronts of the Socialist Revolution . . . launched the "Big Leap Forward" program for economic development and established people's communes throughout the nation's agricultural areas. Under these new conditions, the workers and farmers made an urgent demand to raise their educational level. To meet this popular demand, to complete basically the Socialist Revolution, to speed up Socialist construction and to carry out step by step the historical responsibility of technical and cultural revolution, the Central Committee of the Chinese Communist Party and the State Council issued the "Directive concerning educational work." The directive sets down the policy that education must fulfill its political role, must serve the cause of the proletariat, must be combined with productive labor, and finally it must be carried out under the leadership of the Party. The directive further emphasizes the need for improving education quantitatively, qualitatively, speedily, and economically and the need for . . . stimulating and rallying popular support in order to bring about the realization of educational work by the entire Party and by the whole people. Since this policy has been outlined, it has received the wholehearted support of the people of the nation. . . .

Our work in education is one of the powerful instruments of the proletariat to reform the old society and to build a new society. As far back as 1934, Comrade Mao Tse-tung pointed out that the over-all educational and cultural policy was to educate the great laboring masses in the spirit of communism. The objectives were: to place culture and education at the service of the Revolution and class struggle and to link education with the proletariat in order that the whole Chinese people have the opportunity of enjoying culture and happiness. Fundamentally, this policy has been followed since that time up to present. The 1958 educational revolution aims at intensifying the service of education to the cause of socialist revolution and construction, at eliminating what remains of the exploiting class, and at forming the basis for transition to communism. And it aims at erasing the distinction between mental and physical work. Consequently, we must thoroughly and faithfully implement the Party's policy "to foster the moral, intellectual and physical development of those who are being educated, in order that they may become socialism-conscious and cultured workers" . . . a new type of well-rounded persons, who are able to perform mental as well as manual work. We must strive to make intellectuals also laborers and intellectualize workers and peasants.

In addition, the educational revolution has resolved the problem of relationship between education and politics. The bourgeois class hypocritically pretend "education for its own sake," or "students do not mix themselves with politics." We, on the contrary, declare that education must render political service to the proletariat, professional pursuits must be combined with political ideology, and we must produce "red and expert" workers. We make Marxist-Leninist ideological education and the political work of the Party the soul of all activities in schools and let politics take command in all cultural, scientific, and educational endeavors.

We have introduced the systematic study of Marxist-Leninist theory, the study of political and economic conditions and responsibilities of different periods, sanctioned practical training through the participation in various political activities and productve labor, thus dispensing socialist-communist ideological education to teachers and students on a wide scale and on a thoroughgoing basis. In 1958, under the Party leadership, students and teachers carried out widespread debates; by stating realities, expounding logic, criticizing and self criticizing, they thoroughly refuted the bourgeois concept of divorce between work and politics, and as a result of this exercise, they gained greater insight into socialism. The pursuit of individual interest by being "expert but not red" or "white experts" characterized by bourgeois individualism was severely denounced by the masses. Equipping oneself with the proletariat world view and "becoming the intelligentsia of the working class" became the firm aspiration of students and teachers.

The essence of the Educational Revolution consists of combining education with labor; this has great historical significance. Ever since humanity has entered class societies, education by the exploiting classes has a common characteristic: separation of education from productive labor and contempt for physical labor and the spirit behind it. They dispense partial knowledge to those they educate. Unless such tradition is overthrown, unless education is combined with productive labor, we cannot hope to produce "socialism-conscious and cultured workers"; neither can education render political service to the proletariat.

. . . Realizing the importance of this policy, the great masses of students, in the spring of 1958, under the leadership of the Party, began to take part in productive activities. . . . Teachers and students of secondary schools and above formed groups to .work in factories, mines, farms, and in road construction. They lived, ate, and worked with workers and farmers and learned from them. . . . Pupils and teachers of elementary schools took part in welfare work to the extent of their abilities. Just before the summer vacation, under the Party appeal to "suppress superstition and liberate thought" and inspired by the gigantic efforts being made by the worker-peasant masses, students and teachers displayed the communist spirit of "daring to think, to speak and to act"; a drive to establish factories and farms was launched by schools of various levels. Students and teachers did everything themselves, while establishing co-operation with factories. . . . If lacking skills, they learned while working; if facilities were limited, they accommodated to the fullest extent, thus confronting the criticism of onlookers with realistic accomplishments. Frequently, after a few days and nights of work, a school would set up several scores of large and small factories, garages, and workshops. While this was going on, normal schools and colleges engaged in setting up spare-time schools; medical schools engaged in establishing hospitals and clinics. Everyone took pride in being able to serve the working class and contribute to the development of the national economy. During the people's iron-steel drive, 90,000 science and engineering students, together with their younger instructors, systematically organized themselves to actively participate in the drive. . . . They helped to locate ores, select and analyze ores, produce iron and steel, make and install machineries . . . and in planning. . . . Thus, inside the furnace steel was being made and outside the furnace men were being trained. . . .

\*    \*    \*

. . . At the appropriate time, the Party Central Committee and the State Council summed up this popular experience and issued lines of orientation. The salient points are: in establishing factories and farms, schools should not only aim at producing a new type of citizen, but should also experiment with and produce new goods; factories and people's communes, in running schools, should not only concern themselves with producing goods, but should also take the responsibility of cultivating the new type of citizen. There are three types of schools: full-time schools, part-time schools, and spare-time schools.

All types of schools at all levels must make productive labor an integral part of their curriculum and included in their educational plan. In full-time schools, study is the main concern; students must, however, regularly take part in productive labor which, as far as possible, should be connected with their fields of specialization. In part-time schools, students devote half-time to study and half-time to work, or alternate work with study every other day or every other week. They are students, but also workers or farmers. There are three forms of student participation in labor: (a) in school-established factories or farms—this makes for ease of curriculum planning and of making productive labor a regular part of the curriculum; (b) co-operate with factories or people's communes or work in them under contract—this form offers the advantage of direct contact with worker-peasant masses and expands the teachers' and students' horizon; (c) participate in social welfare work—a specially good way to cultivate the communist attitude toward labor, that of contributing toward public welfare regardless of remuneration. All three forms have their place; none should be neglected in favor of the others. In the various types of spare-time schools, the study should obey the dictates of production. Thus, education is combined with labor and labor is combined with education. . . .

* * *

The existence of a society is determined by the social consciousness of its members. Students actively engaged in labor come in close contact with workers and peasants. There first appears in them a profound spiritual and physical transformation. Through this experience, they become educated in the standpoint of the proletariat, of labor, of the masses, of collectivity, and even in the point of view of dialectic materialism. Through actual participation in the creation of material and spiritual riches, they come to appreciate the greatness of labor and its true role in constructing society. . . . This is living education. This experience not only increases students' respect for the working class, their identification with it, but also makes them understand the power of solidarity and the importance of discipline. "They have calluses on their hands, but they have changed their standpoint; their skin has been darkened by sunshine, their thinking has been reddened. . . ." Today's students are no longer regarded by the worker-peasant masses as "the book learners, who do not move their hands or feet and are incapable of distinguishing the various kinds of grains." On the contrary, they now regard the students as the intelligentsia of their own. They would say, "We used to worry which side you would take after you had gone to school, now we are sure."

Combining education with labor means better integration of theory with practice; this has resulted in greater efficiency in education. Students generally reflect on their learning experiences; after participation in productive labor, they have greater sensitivity, new insights and deepened understanding of theoretical studies. They learn and retain more rapidly and have greater ability for individual work. This is particularly true of those in secondary and higher professional schools. This method of education is far superior to the abstract lectures in classrooms. . . . In the past, practical training in production did not place stress on the end result of production; work was not carried out in a serious atmosphere and there were frequent inaccuracies. Today, in paying attention to the end products, a complete change has taken place; the attitude toward work and professional standards have tremendously improved. In the past, in lesson planning and planning for graduation theses, questions and problems were pure inventions; they bore no relation to reality. . . . At present, suitable practical and concrete problems are selected to the fullest extent. . . . For the most part, students work on different projects in rotation, mutually verify each other's work, and discuss in larger groups; thus they are able to grasp the problem as a whole and the relative importance of the parts. This form of study has been widely recognized as the best method to integrate theory and practice; it provides the opportunity of linking mathematics[3] with production and scientific research, far superior to abstract conjectural problems. . . .

. . . As a result of students and teachers actively participating in productive labor, they discovered for themselves many scientific and technical problems urgently needing attention. This set off a movement of scientific research in higher education institutions in the latter part of 1958. Under the Party leadership and in cognizance of the importance of linking theory with practice and the direction of research activities in the service of socialist construction . . . the researchers have maintained close contact with the masses and eliminated in them the blind superstitions of exclusiveness of expertness and the attitude of awe toward scientific research. They have thus succeeded in correcting the misconception of a small number of experts working in isolation for their personal gain, and the former divorce between research and reality. . . . During the past few months, the number of research projects undertaken compared with the previous year was tenfold; the quality of work has also considerably improved. The outcome of these projects has not only brought solutions to the many problems of national economy . . . but has also fostered the emergence of a new type of "expert and red" person.

\*    \*    \*

The educational revolution started in 1958 thoroughly implemented the Party's policy of "walking on two legs." [This consists of] stimulating the masses and relying on their support—making education the responsibility of the entire Party and of the entire people. Under the principle of combining unity with diversity, expansion with higher standards, national over-all planning with local rights and responsibilities, national schools are developed side by side with schools maintained by factories, indus-

3 TRANSLATOR'S NOTE: In a later paragraph, not included in this translation, reference is made to the improvement of teaching mathematics in elementary and secondary schools. This apparently was a problem area.

tries, and people's communes; regular schools and professional training are simultaneously developed; adult education and child education are given equal importance; full-time, part-time, and spare-time schools are each given their appropriate place; school education and self education (including correspondence and broadcast schools) are carried on at the same time; free education and paid education exist alongside of one another. Thus, education is developed to the fullest extent. While the Government was extending educational facilities, factories, mines, enterprises, and people's communes set out to establish their own schools. Workers and peasants . . . supplied free labor and materials to build schools and contribute to their finance. The problem of teachers was solved by recruiting locally persons who are capable to teach. Thus, in the short span of a few months, several hundreds of thousands of spare-time schools of various types and levels, as well as several scores of thousands of half-day secondary agricultural schools and regular secondary, elementary schools, and pre-schools, have come into being throughout the nation. The majority of localities have now achieved the fundamental aim of an elementary school and nurseries in each section of the people's commune, a lower secondary school in each commune, and a higher secondary in each county. Special districts are equipped with secondary professional schools and specialized schools. Every province, municipality, and autonomous district possesses higher education institutions of various types. . . . Our educational work has truly become the business of the people, truly serving the interest of the working class and truly in the hands of the people. The expansion of education among the laboring class bears great significance to the development of socialism and the furtherance of national construction. . . .

* * *

. . . The victory of the 1958 Educational Revolution is due to the Party's correct leadership, and this victory has consolidated the Party leadership in the development of education. . . .

Socialist education must be carried out under Party leadership, for socialist education is a powerful instrument of the proletariat for the reconstruction of mankind and nature. It is an integral part of the Socialist Revolution and socialist construction. Educational work is inseparable from political and economic activities, and without Party leadership it is apt to lose its orientation and fail to serve socialism. The Central Committee of the Party, the State Council, and Comrade Mao Tse-tung have imaginatively applied Marxist-Leninist educational theory, brought together the rich experience of the Chinese Revolution, and have evolved a whole body of systematic policy and methods, as well as an integral educational system. . . .

. . . In order to strengthen educational leadership, the Party Central Committee and the Party representatives at different levels have applied systematic measures: conferences are called to discuss progress, repeated propaganda is made of the Party's educational policy, investigations conducted to inquire into the practical conditions for the implementation of the policy, evaluations are made of experiences, solutions are introduced as needed. The Party secretaries[4] are given the position of command . . . a large number of cadres equipped with long-term training in revolutionary struggle have been assigned to schools of various levels for leadership work. In higher education institutions, the system of a school-affairs committee under the guidance of a Party representative has been introduced to provide the impetus to strengthen ideological education, teaching and research activities, and to ensure the faithful implementation of the Party's policy. . . .

\* \* \*

Our educational work, through 10 years' development, especially the 1958 revolution, has achieved great victory

4 TRANSLATOR'S NOTE: This refers to the secretaries of Communist committees at different levels.

and gained rich experience. Educational workers throughout the nation must . . . continue this effort with increased vigor, scrutinize and uproot all rightist ideas. Where illiteracy has been eradicated, and elementary and lower middle schools universalized, attention should be given to . . . raising the qualitative level of education and to developing a number of model schools. Full-time schools, while trying to raise standards, must not be slack in productive labor. Higher education institutions must further develop research activities in line with the requirements of national economy. Further, the movement for the eradication of illiteracy must be pushed ahead and the spare-time schools for workers and peasants well administered. We must learn, on a continuous basis, the lessons taught by experience and to overcome the weaknesses in our work. . . . We must continue to push ahead the Educational Revolution, speedily complete our cultural revolution, achieve universal education, and cultivate a full rank of red and expert proletarian intelligentsia. These are our historical duties . . . the accomplishment of which will reveal our country as a highly cultured people in the world.

# 10: Down with the Fountainhead of Revisionist Education

*The following article by Shih Yen-hung appeared in* Jen-min jih-pao (People's Daily) *on July 18, 1967.*

Throughout the seventeen years since the founding of the People's Republic, a sharp and bitter struggle between two classes and between two policy lines has persisted on the educational front, as it has on the economic and political fronts. Chairman Mao formulated for the proletariat a revolutionary road for socialist education. On the other hand, the leading power-holder in the party who follows a capitalist road [Liu Shao-chi] has stubbornly—and with the great powers of the state and the party at his disposal—pursued a long and wide road of counterrevolutionary revisionism in the field of education. These are two fundamentally opposing roads. Whereas the former is designed to serve and safeguard the interest of proletarian dictatorship, the latter is designed to bring about a restoration of capitalism. Whereas the former is designed to cultivate the successors to take over the proletarian revolution, the latter is aimed at the preservation of the landlord and bourgeois classes.

The leading power-holder in the party who follows a capitalist road is the fountainhead and mainstay of the revisionist educational road. In these seventeen years, this Khrushchev of China has considered education a means to his goal of seizing supreme power of the armed forces and the state machine. He has gathered a small group of counterrevolutionary revisionists and stationed them in the field of education to resist fanatically the proletarian educational policy line of Chairman Mao. Now is the time for us to uproot thoroughly the counter-revolutionary revisionist educational line and to crush completely the fountainhead and the major behind-the-scenes supporter of that policy line.

## GUARDIAN ANGEL OF THE OLD EDUCATIONAL SYSTEM

In 1949, New China rose in the East like a giant. Where was this New China headed? Our great leader, Chairman Mao, pointed out clearly: the Chinese revolution "will not and cannot build a bourgeois society of Chinese bourgeois dictatorship." It can only "build a Chinese socialist society." But the leading power-holder in the party who follows a capitalist road advocated the policy of "consolidating the new democratic order," clamoring that capitalists "made their contributions through exploitation." His wanton hope was to topple the proletarian dictatorship and to establish capitalism.

This conflict showed itself on the educational front, where an acute struggle between socialist and capitalist lines has been joined.

In the early years of the People's Republic, there were two distinctly different types of educational systems. One was the new educational system of the long-liberated areas. It had been developed under the personal leadership of Chairman Mao. First, there were classes and lectures conducted by the peasant movement institutes during the first civil war period [1924–1931]. Then there were the Yenan Anti-Japanese Military and Political Academy, guided personally by Comrade Lin Piao during the Sino-Japanese War, and the many other schools which followed the revolutionary traditions of their predecessors. These institutions all stood for a brand-new kind of revolutionary and proletarian education. They turned out large numbers of revolutionary cadres. As

early as 1934, Chairman Mao set forth this basic principle of proletarian education: "To educate the broad
working masses in the communist spirit; to cultivate and
educate to serve the interest of revolutionary warfare
and the class struggle; to integrate education and labor;
and to bless the broad masses in China with culture and
well-being." The essence of this principle is: education
must serve the interest of proletarian seizure of national
power.

The other was the old education system left over from
the days of the Kuomintang reactionary rule. This system served the interests and helped perpetuate the position of the landlord and bourgeois classes, of imperialist
reactionary rule, and of the system of exploitation.

In terms of quantity, the difference between these two
systems was pronounced. For example, in higher education, the new education of the liberated areas encom-
passed only 15 per cent of the enrollment, while the old
education in the formerly Kuomintang-ruled areas 85
per cent.

Under these circumstances, a crucial question arose on
the educational front: should we transform the old on
the basis of the new revolutionary proletarian education
in order to consolidate the proletarian dictatorship? Or
should we let the old education of the landlord and
bourgeois classes remain unchanged to serve the interest
of capitalism and to bring about an overthrow of the
proletarian dictatorship?

Chairman Mao has told us to "carefully change old
educational institutions one step at a time" on the basis
of the experiences gained in new education in old liberated areas. He has clearly pointed out: "In dealing
with this problem, it is wrong either to procrastinate because of a reluctance to reform, or to rashly push
through reforms with brutal force and high-handed
methods." In the early years of the People's Republic,
in response to the call and leadership of Chairman Mao,
education in China not only grew quantitatively, but
also underwent some reforms.

But the leading power-holder in the party who took the capitalist road publicly resisted and spurned Chairman Mao's instructions. On the one hand, he did his best to deprecate education in the old liberated areas. For example, he falsely branded such schools as the Anti-Japanese College as "a training class" and "not a college in the normal sense." He even attacked as "outdated" and "must be cast away" the principles laid down personally by Chairman Mao on which the Anti-Japanese College was founded. On the other hand, he commended highly the schools built by imperialists in China for the purpose of waging cultural aggression. He said that such colleges, "established with the experiences of Western Europe, Britain, the United States, France, and Japan, had their merits in raising the cultural, scientific, and knowledge levels of the Chinese people." Unashamedly, he said: "No matter, if it is a foreigner, a capitalist, or all the rich men in the world—as long as they are willing to contribute to the building and maintenance of schools, we welcome them. To build and run schools is commendable." These words fully betrayed the true colors of these servile self-styled "red compradors." He said: "If we do not have a history textbook, *Tzu Chih T'ung Chien* [The Comprehensive Mirror for Aid in Government] [1] will do," indicating that we should learn from feudalism. Later, he also attempted to sell a large bill of revisionist goods under the name of "studying the Soviet Union." He issued directives to a small handful of power-holders in the party organization of the Ministry of Education who walk a capitalist path, making clear his wish that "following the Soviets completely and thoroughly" should be the "unshakable policy" of educational reform. In this way all the feudalist, capitalist, and revisionist relics, after a quick change of outer appearances, sallied forth at the green light of "studying the Soviets" in matters ranging from school organization systems, curricula,

[1] [A well-known Chinese historical publication by Ssu-ma Kuang (1018–1086), a statesman of the Sung Dynasty. The publication is a comprehensive history of China covering the years 403 B.C. to 919 A.D. in 294 chapters.]

contents of courses, and teaching methods to the administering of examinations.

Publicly, the Khrushchev of China also resisted Chairman Mao's following directive: "The goal of our education effort should be the development of the educated in all these directions, such as morality, mental capability, and physical fitness, so that they may become cultured and socialistically enlightened workers." And he shamelessly tried to instill the commercial and venal philosophy of "climbing upward" into the minds of youths. He called on the students "to earnestly tackle their tasks," "to try hard to turn themselves into 'red specialists.'" He also coaxed them: "If you study one specialty real well, you will one day become a famous specialist and you will have everything you want." In accordance with these instructions, a small handful of power-holders in the party organizations of the Ministry of Education drafted "Regulations Governing the Conferring of Academic Degrees, Titles, and Other Honors" and "Regulations Governing the Cultivation of Vice Doctors and Research Fellows." Their aim was to lure youths with the bait of fame and profit, and turn them into successors for the bourgeois class.

Under these circumstances, even some of the schools in the old liberated areas which had a revolutionary tradition gradually discarded the tradition and joined the ranks of the feudalist, capitalist, and revisionist camp. Some revolutionary colleges, originally patterned after the Anti-Japanese College, were turned into such "most scientific, most advanced new standard and normal colleges" as Moscow University. Such conversions were no surprise. That was precisely what the Khrushchev of China intended to do with education.

As a result of the struggle between two opposing lines on the educational front after the founding of the People's Republic, reactionary old education gobbled up revolutionary new education. This was precisely the result of a fanatic struggle against the proletarian educational line of Chairman Mao. This struggle was staged by the leading power-holder in the party who follows a capitalist road and who has assigned himself as the guardian angel of the old educational system.

## COMMANDER OF REACTIONARY COUNTERATTACK

In 1958, a great educational revolution of unprecedented fury, momentum, and influence broke out in our country. This revolution was caused by the profound changes brought to the nation's political and economic arena by the three "Red Banners" of Chairman Mao. It was also the result of "the spirit of communism blooming vigorously throughout the land," and of the destruction of all the shackles of revisionism on education. In this same year, Chairman Mao laid down the principle that education should serve the interest of proletarian politics, and that education should be integrated with productive labor. An overwhelming tide of the great educational revolution swept through the country with thunderous force and fury.

Ever since the workers, peasants, and soldiers took the unprecedented step of taking over the field of education, this great educational revolution was their first attempt at improving the situation. Various types of schools mushroomed under their auspices. The monopoly of bourgeois intellectuals was broken. Torrents of criticism were directed at the old feudalist, capitalist, and revisionist education system, which hid behind the name of "learning from the Soviets." The reactionary academic "authorities," who had lorded over the field, were suddenly deprived of all their prestige and luster. The great educational revolution represented changes in teaching and learning unknown to our history, changes which affected school organization systems, curricula, the contents of courses, and instruction methods on a wholesale scale. Factory and farm work became an important part of the schools. And teachers and students walked out of their book-lined studies into the three great revolutionary movements and into close association and integration with the worker and peasant masses.

The leading power-holder in the party who follows a capitalist road is extremely hostile toward the great educational revolution. When this revolution was being developed enthusiastically and noisily, he poured cold water on it and denounced it as "possibly having the effect of downgrading the quality of learning." He even assailed the principle laid down by Chairman Mao for the great educational revolution, alleging that "the goals and principles of education were not clearly delineated in the past" and there should be "criticism." Later, he continued his insidious barrage against the "revolution of empty talk and the revolution in quotation marks," denouncing the great revolution on the cultural and educational front as "deviation." He even directed his darts against the party's central authorities led by Chairman Mao, cursing that "the party will fall if this situation continues."

From 1960 to 1962, taking advantage of an anti-China and anticommunist campaign launched by class enemies at home and abroad, the Khrushchev of China made his frenetic assaults on the party, socialism, and Mao Tse-tung's thought. On the educational front, he ganged up with such counterrevolutionary revisionists as Lu Ting-yi to energetically push for a capitalist comeback under the guise of "correcting" the "deviations" in the great educational revolution and "upgrading the quality of teaching." Painstakingly, they "summarized" the experiences of the "big-name" universities of the warlord and Kuomintang days; they mixed them with the haphazardly purloined educational experiences of British and American imperialists and of Soviet revisionists, and with tidbits of feudalist, capitalist, and revisionist education; and they dressed the final product in a Marxist–Leninist outer garb. This was then fraudulently represented as the overall summation of the decades of educational experiences of New China. They had, of course, the whole works—from school organization systems, curricula, textbooks, and school rules and regulations—oriented in their direction, and they were forcing them down the throats of the educators. Some of the typical orders were: "Sixty

Requirements for Higher Education," "Fifty Requirements for Middle Schools," and "Forty Requirements for
Elementary Schools." These counterrevolutionary and
revisionist principles were handed down by the Khrushchev of China as the ordained "basic laws" to be absolutely, unconditionally, and thoroughly carried out by
the educational institutions on all levels. In this way the
old educational system of pre-1958 vintage was given
complete sanction in theory and in law, and completely
systematized and institutionalized.

These multi-point principles and programs invariably
underscored the need "to maintain normal order in the
school" and to negate and discredit the results of the
great educational revolution. They emphasized strongly
that "moral education comes first" and "technology
reigns supreme." They refuted the need of subjecting all
fields in the school and in the educational system to the
rule of Mao Tse-tung's thought; opposed to revolution-
izing the minds of men; and they completely failed to
recognize the struggle to be waged inside the schools to
crush capitalism and to promote the victory of the proletariat.

The Khrushchev of China and his followers secretly
planned to advance the so-called "small pagoda" theory
for the development of education and the organization
of school systems. This "small pagoda" theory was a copy
and extension of the capitalist practice of running "educational stores." In this business, the capitalist managers
adopted a system of elimination. The overwhelming majority of the students were eliminated, leaving only a
very small number to climb the school ladder higher and
higher. The Khrushchev of China stressed so-called "selected education" and advocated that "one or two universities should be well-maintained and some excellent
students recruited for advanced studies." "If they study
a number of years, let them study that many years. The
quality of learning must be maintained at a high level."
Underneath these words was the intention of preparing
a group of mental and intellectual aristocracy for a capitalist comeback. The eight-year college is an example of

such schools, which inherited completely "to the last drop" the educational experiences of the American imperialists. They left behind the eight-year school system, the bourgeois control of educational institutions, the system of student elimination, the tutor system, and education for the gifted. All the substance and trimmings of imperialist education were taken over whole hog. As a result, this institution turned out a total of some fifty students in more than seven years. Poisoned by this educational system, many of these students, in pursuit of personal fame and profit, became "specialists" and "professors," and they looked down grumpily on services to the workers and farmers in the factory and on the farm.

The many kinds of schools established by the workers and farmers in the high tide of the great educational revolution were ruthlessly stamped out if they failed to meet the requirements set down by the Khrushchev of China. For instance, incomplete statistics showed that in 1962 there were 22,600 agricultural middle schools, with an enrollment of some 2,300,000. Now only 3,715 such schools are left, with an enrollment of 266,000. The same fate befell the elementary schools. In 1958, some 83 per cent of school-age children were in school. This was drastically cut down to 56.1 per cent. Large numbers of children of workers and farmers have been expelled from schools.

The laws promulgated by the Khrushchev of China stipulated that the party merely "supervises and provides guarantees and assurances" in schools. He once expressed the toughness of his position in saying: "We do want to deprive the party branch office of the leadership position" in the school and turn over the power of education to bourgeois intellectuals. It was he who slanderously described the struggle against the reactionary and bourgeois "authorities" in the great educational revolution as "a bedlam of name-calling." And it was also he who took off the "hats" of bourgeois intellectuals and gave them instead the title of "working intellectuals rendering services to socialism," thus vastly raising the status of these bourgeois intellectuals. These reactionary bourgeois academic "authorities" wantonly and arrogantly proclaimed: "Since 1958, the young actors have had their shows in the schools. Now it is time for us, the old, to make our appearance." These monstrosities usurped great powers in the field of education and ruthlessly imposed a bourgeois dictatorship. They literally turned schools into the forward bases of a capitalist resurrection. Just as Chairman Mao pointed out to us: "If things continue to go this way, it would not take long—several or a dozen years, and at the most several dozen years—for the reactionary to stage a nationwide comeback, an inevitable comeback. The Marxist–Leninist party will surely become a revisionist party and a fascist party. The whole of China will change color."

## MASTER OF PSEUDOCOMMUNISM

In 1962, Chairman Mao sounded his great bugle call at the Eighth Session of the Tenth Plenum, admonishing us "to make absolutely sure not to forget the class struggle." This call touched off the counterattack by the proletariat in the ideological arena.

From the fifties to the sixties, the class struggle at home and abroad has become increasingly acute. In the international communist movement, many proletarian political parties and socialist countries have undergone a change in nature and strayed on a revisionist path. The Soviet Union's Communist Party, founded personally by Lenin, has been changed into a revisionist party. The world's first socialist country has become a country of bourgeois dictatorship. This extremely sad development is an alarm for all revolutionary peoples throughout the world. In our country, after the fundamental reform was completed—in accordance with the socialist principle governing the means of production—an undercurrent of capitalist restoration also surfaced within our party. How can China forestall this change of color? How can the Chinese Communist Party prevent itself from changing into a revisionist party? These are the most important questions being asked by the proletarian class and by revolutionary peoples throughout the world.

The great Chinese Communist Party, led by the genius, our leader Chairman Mao, and armed by the ever-triumphant thought of Mao Tse-tung, can give these questions a satisfactory answer. Completely, systematically, and scientifically, Chairman Mao expounded the theories of socialist social classes, class contradictions, and class struggle. He laid down the guidelines, the principles, and policies of how to wage a revolution under proletarian dictatorship. And he advanced Marxism–Leninism to a brand-new stage of development, the thought of Mao Tse-tung stage of development.

The struggle to win over the younger generation is a struggle of monumental importance to the life and death of our party and our country. Chairman Mao has told us to cultivate and educate—at the very height of the storm—hundreds of thousands of successors for our proletarian revolution. In 1964, after the Spring Festival, Chairman Mao personally directed the polarized struggle on the educational front, and issued instructions several times in connection with educational work.

Chairman Mao has taught us: "All the moribund reactionary forces in man's history invariably stage their last struggles against the forces of revolution." "When placed in a disadvantageous position, representatives of the various exploiter classes often take the offensive in order to defensively preserve their own existence or to develop future benefit." The leading power-holder in the party who follows a capitalist road has long hidden himself behind the scenes. Now he saw the tide turning against him, and he became worried and even desperate. Suddenly he catapulted himself onto the stage. Less than three months after Chairman Mao issued his Spring Festival instructions, this power-holder put forward a self-styled communist theory: "Two labor systems and two educational systems." This was his attempt at prolonging the stubborn fight against the proletariat. His aim was to preserve the reactionary forces of the bourgeois class on the educational front and to restore capitalism in China.

The Chinese Khrushchev represented his concoction of "two labor systems and two educational systems" as one of three great steps taken in the field of "defense preparations." In another direction, he also turned to organizational methods and established an "Educational Directory" under his own command. To organize his following, he ordered "The Second Education Ministry," "The Second Education Commission," and "The Second Education Bureau" to be formed on various levels of government. Bare-handed, this Khrushchev of China plunged into the fray. He toured more than a dozen cities and provinces in the country and wrote more than twenty reports. Within one year, he called five national conventions under the nominal auspices of the Ministry of Education, the Ministry of Higher Education, the Ministry of Agriculture, and the Ministry of Hygiene. His followers and associates—such as P'eng Chen, Lu Ting-i, and Chiang—trekked all over the country in an announced effort to make this "inventor" of the "two educational systems" a well-known name in every household. While building up his personal prestige, this Chinese Khrushchev was at the same time baring his teeth and directing his spears at our great leader, Chairman Mao. He shouted: "We'll create a situation in which we can defeat you and remove your leader," or "If you hold the power, so can I." How arrogant was the Chinese Khrushchev! How furious his fire of counterrevolution!

What are, after all, the "two educational systems"? This is the theory and explanation advanced by the Chinese Khrushchev himself: "Our country should have two educational systems. One is the whole-day, full-time school educational system." "This whole-day school system cannot be abridged." "It probably would take one hundred, two hundred, or three hundred years." The other system is the "half-work and half-study school system" which "must be developed vigorously." Clearly, the "two educational systems" mean the full-time system plus the half-work and half-study system. Why did the Khrushchev of China play with this concoction? He said: "If one cannot afford to go to a full-time school, he goes to a half-day school. There is so much to be done in a full-time school. Sometimes one can only go to a half-day school." Chiang, his follower, was more blunt about it. He said: "If you can afford it, go to a college; or else go to the farm." What they said was that the full-time school system educates the minority into spiritual aristocrats, while half-day schools are used to meet the needs of the workers, the lower poor peasants, and their children who "cannot afford" to go to the former. They are to be educated and trained into "common workers and peasants" to be ordered around.

Half-work and half-study is a method proposed by our great leader, Chairman Mao. The leading power-holder in the party who follows a capitalist road purloined this great method and altered it to suit his own campaign of selling his revisionist wares.

The so-called "half-work and half-study," as proposed by the Chinese Khrushchev, was nothing more than truncating the full-time school system and making up [the time] with labor. This was completely contradictory to Chairman Mao's instructions that education should serve the interest of proletarian politics and should help revolutionize the mind of man. The revisionist "half-study" was the same as study under the whole-day system, where students stuffed themselves with books that were contradictory to Mao Tse-tung's thought and divorced from the work and experiences of the three great revolutions. The "half-work" was no more than putting him to work as a member of the labor force. These were still the old roads in the old educational system, where bourgeois intellectuals lorded over the schools. There, "mental cultivation comes first" and "technology reigns supreme." Was there even a breath of communist education?

Some half-work and half-study schools completely failed to heed the educational policy lines laid down by Chairman Mao; they forgot entirely about the class struggle between the proletariat and the bourgeois class. In them, only such a "school tradition" of "plunging headlong into studies and putting all you have in the work" is emphasized. Most of the time, students were treated merely as a labor force working in the factories. For the small remaining portion of time they were taught the isolated tidbits of book knowledge under the full-time system. The goal was merely to train workers of certain grades. Such a school was the red banner institution advocated and personally built with such fanfare by the Khrushchev of China!

In a word, the half-work and half-study school perceived by the Khrushchev of China was nothing but the vocational school under bourgeois rule. His "two educational systems" were nothing more than a duplicate of the capitalist dual system of "education of talent" and "education for the workers." He wished to pass his "two educational systems" for communist education; and he actually described them as "a development of Marxism–Leninism" that was of "great international significance." It was utterly ridiculous!

His "two educational systems" provide for the rich to go to the full-time schools where "specialists are cultivated," while sending the poor, the children of the lower middle poor farmers and workers, to the half-work and half-study schools where "the common workers and farmers are trained." This way, not only would we fail to narrow the "three great differences," but there will also be a sharpening of the division between classes.

His "two educational systems" did not require the students to arm themselves with Mao Tse-tung's thought and to turn consciously toward revolution. They only urged the students to "be able to engage both in the labor of the mind and the labor of the body." Students turned out by these schools would never be the "all-round new men" needed by the proletarian class, but would emerge as revisionist seedlings, knowing nothing but technology and climbing upward only by means of technical excellence.

His "two educational systems" made no mention of the two classes and two lines and of the struggle between the classes and policy lines. They also failed to acknowledge the need to strengthen and consolidate the proletarian dictatorship. The theme was "half-work and half-study is in itself a class struggle." The aim was to lure people to education for education's sake. This could not "prevent capitalism from staging a comeback." On the contrary, this actually paved the way for the restoration of capitalism in China.

From all that can be seen, the "two educational systems"—emphasized and publicized so much by the Khrushchev of China—could not "eradicate the three great differences" as they were claimed to be capable of. The truth turned out to be that, if anything, the two systems widened the three great differences. They did not and could not "cultivate the all-round new men of communism," but only turned out the successors for the bourgeois class. They could not "prevent capitalism from staging a comeback," but actually helped pave the way for a restoration of capitalism in China.

In a nutshell, the "two educational systems" presented by the leading power-holder inside the party who follows a capitalist road was the reflection of his political line on the educational front. That political line called for the renunciation of class struggles and of proletarian dictatorship in order that the world would "grow" peacefully into communism.

It is clear for all to see that the Khrushchev in China is the great master of all of pseudocommunist education.

In a letter to Comrade Lin Piao, Chairman Mao wrote on May 7, 1966, that "the students' main task is to study, but they should also learn other things. They should study not only literature, but also industry, agriculture, and military affairs, and criticize the bourgeoisie. The period of schooling must be shortened and education must be revolutionized. The atmosphere in which the bourgeois intellectuals control our schools must not be allowed to continue any longer." These "May 7" instructions by Chairman Mao are the highest directives for our efforts in education. It is a formally announced death sentence for the "two educational systems" advanced by the Khrushchev of China, and for the counterrevolutionary revisionist education policy line and the old educational system pursued by him through the seventeen years since liberation.

The tumultuous and momentous Great Proletarian Cultural Revolution roars on with the thunderous fury of a mountainous tidal wave, washing and sweeping away all the puddles of stagnant water left behind by the old society. The positions on the educational front, as well as on all other fronts, that were under the control of the Khrushchev of China have been retaken, one after another, by the proletariat. The Khrushchev of China and his paraphernalia of revisionist wares were exposed and brought to public scrutiny and scorn. This was a resounding victory for the Great Proletarian Cultural Revolution and a great triumph for Mao Tse-tung's thought.

Let us hold high the great red flag of Mao Tse-tung's thought and fight the fountainhead and main behind-the-scenes supporter of the counterrevolutionary revisionist educational policy line until it is defeated and its notoriety becomes widely known. Our criticism must be merciless and thoroughgoing. We must destroy the last vestiges of the exploiter class educational system that has reigned for thousands of years since the time of Confucius. We must turn our schools into the great institutions of Mao Tse-tung's thought. We must ensure that our future generations remain of sterling qualities forever and ever, and our land thoroughly and completely red forever and ever.

## 11: The Way to Train Engineering and Technical Personnel As Viewed from the Shanghai Machine Tool Plant

*The article which follows is an investigation report written by correspondents of* Wen-hui pao *and the New China News Agency. It appeared in* Jen-min jih-pao (People's Daily) *on July 22, 1968.*

### NOTE BY EDITOR OF PEOPLE'S DAILY

We recommend the following investigation report to all proletarian revolutionary comrades, broad masses of workers, poor and lower-middle peasants, student youths, revolutionary intellectuals, and revolutionary cadres in the nation. This report vividly describes how the Great Proletarian Cultural Revolution has produced a great change in the ranks of engineering and technical personnel and has demonstrated the great vitality of new socialist ideas. It is entitled "The Way to Train Engineering and Technical Personnel as Viewed from the Shanghai Machine Tool Plant," but it also points out the revolutionary direction of school education.

Recently, Chairman Mao thoughtfully pointed out: "It is still necessary to have universities; here I refer mainly to colleges of science and engineering. However, it is essential to shorten the period of schooling, revolutionize education, put proletarian politics in command,

and follow the road of the Shanghai Machine Tool Plant in training technicians from among the workers. Students should be selected from among workers and peasants with practical experience and they should return to production work after a few years' study."

This great call of Chairman Mao is our battle order to carry the proletarian educational revolution to the end. It is the great "antirevisionist" plan for the next hundred years. All true proletarian revolutionary comrades in revolutionary committees at all levels, factories, and schools, and on all other fronts in the country must firmly follow Chairman Mao's policy on proletarian education. They must criticize the revisionist education policy and destroy the old bourgeois educational system. And they must resolutely follow the worker–peasant–soldier road, as pointed out by Chairman Mao, in order to carry through the educational revolution to the end.

Scientific research departments and leading organs should also carefully study this report, for it is a sharp weapon to further criticize the antirevolutionary revisionist policy on science and technology advocated by China's Khrushchev.

The great historical significance of the Great Proletarian Cultural Revolution and its far-reaching impact on various aspects of our nation have just begun to be evident. The Great Proletarian Cultural Revolution is the prerequisite for a new industrial revolution in the nation. The tremendous creative force of the masses of people will continuously produce many miracles that the bourgeois fools and the rightist conservatives have never thought of. We would like to advise those near-sighted capitalist followers who have not yet become hopeless diehards to look ahead a bit further. We also would like to advise those college and university students who look down upon workers and peasants, and who think they themselves are so important, to discard their privileged status, so as to quickly catch up with the millions of revolutionary people who are heroically moving forward.

## THE GREAT PROLETARIAN CULTURAL REVOLUTION HAS PRODUCED A PROFOUND CHANGE

The Shanghai Machine Tool Plant is a large factory known for its production of precision grinders. It has over six hundred engineers and technicians. There are three groups of personnel: 45 per cent are technicians promoted from among the workers, 50 per cent are post-liberation college graduates assigned to the plant, and the rest are old technicians who remained after the liberation. The storm of the Great Proletarian Cultural Revolution has produced a profound change in the technical work force at the plant. Primarily, this great revolutionary change is evidenced in the following ways:

1. The proletarian revolutionaries have actual control of the factory, including control over technical decisions. The reactionary bourgeois technical "authorities" who previously controlled the technical leadership of the plant have been overthrown. Many technicians who came from the ranks of workers, revolutionary young technicians, and revolutionary cadres have now become the masters of scientific research and technical design. All of them are proletarian revolutionary fighters, with deep class feelings for Chairman Mao and the Communist Party. This revolutionary technical team, which was suppressed in the past, now continuously demonstrates its creative wisdom and technical skill. With unlimited loyalty to Chairman Mao's proletarian revolutionary line, it is ceaselessly climbing new technical heights. During the first half of this year alone, it had already successfully trial-produced ten new models of precision grinders, including four that meet advanced international standards. The high speed and the excellent quality of the production are unprecedented in the history of the plant.

2. The antirevolutionary revisionist line in technical matters, as advocated by China's Khrushchev, and the reactionary bourgeois world outlook have been severely

denounced. As a result, the bourgeois technical "authorities" have become politically bankrupt, and the true "paper tiger" nature of their technical expertise has been completely exposed. Previously, the capitalist leaders did their best to build up these reactionary "authorities" and "idols" for young technicians to worship and urged them to "measure up" to these "authorities" and to "struggle hard to become engineers." Now, many of these young technicians have greatly changed their outlook. They realize that the idea of having fame and wealth is the beginning of revisionism and that the title of the bourgeois is something that they should not fight for. In the past, not a few researchers in the Grinder Research Department used to record technical data in their personal notebooks, which they treated as their "little private depositories"; but now, at their own initiative, they quickly submit such data to the department and compile them into handbooks for everybody's use. All technicians in the plant have volunteered to work in the shops alongside of the workers and to collaborate with workers in research and in improvement of designs. The old technicians, when they work in the shops, have also made conscientious efforts to shake off their pretentious manners and to humbly learn from the workers.

3. The relations between workers and technicians have changed. In the past, a handful of capitalist roaders and reactionary "authorities" in the plant proposed a so-called "one and one" combination system—that is, one worker serves under one technician. This so-called "combination" meant that "the engineer works with his mouth and the worker with his hands," or the "engineer provides the idea, and the worker does what he is told to do"; and all this was nothing more than the old line that "mental workers rule, and manual workers are ruled." They also preached such reactionary theories as "workers and technicians must check on each other" and "workers and technicians must form two opposite groups." They put into effect a set of rules and systems that were designed to control, check on, and suppress

the workers. The "Handbook for a Productive Worker" alone has over one hundred seventy rules, which every worker had to memorize and follow. All this further widened the vast gap between workers and technicians. During the Great Cultural Revolution, this plant introduced a "three-in-one" combination system, consisting of workers, revolutionary technicians, and revolutionary cadres. Under this system, the ordinary workers now take part in designing, and the technicians also work on the production lines. Because theory and practical work have been closely integrated, the relations between workers and technicians have improved a great deal.

## THE WAY TO TRAIN ENGINEERING AND TECHNICAL PERSONNEL

Young technicians at the Shanghai Machine Tool Plant (including personnel up to about thirty-five years of age) come from two sources: college and university graduates (numbering about three hundred fifty, of whom 10 per cent are postgraduates or those who had studied abroad) and technicians promoted from among the workers (numbering about two hundred fifty, a few of whom had studied at secondary technical schools for a few years). Experience indicates that the latter group is better than the former. Generally, the former group is more backward in its outlook and less competent in actual work. The latter group is more progressive in its ideas, and it is more able. At present, the overwhelming majority of the technicians who came from the ranks of workers are the backbone of the technical work force. And about 10 per cent of them are qualified to independently design high-grade, precision, and advanced new products. Six of the ten new precision grinding machines that were successfully trial-produced during the first half of this year were designed by technicians who came from the workers' ranks.

Promoting technicians from among workers is the way to develop a proletarian engineering and technical work force.

We can see a sharp contrast between two technicians of about the same age, but with different backgrounds:

The first one is a graduate of a university in Shanghai. After one year of study of a foreign language and four years of further study in a foreign country, he received an "Associate Doctor" degree. In 1962, he started to work in the laboratory of the Department of Grinder Research at the plant. Because of the separation of theory from practical work, and because of his failure to collaborate well with workers with some twenty years of school behind him and after a long period of scientific research in the department, he failed to make any outstanding contribution.

The second is a worker. At fourteen, he was an apprentice. At eighteen, he was sent to a machine-building school in Shanghai for four years. In 1957, he was appointed a technician in the Department of Grinder Research. In April of this year, under his direction as the chief designer, a 'large surface grinding machine was successfully trial-produced. This machine, which comes up to advanced international standards, not only meets an urgent need of our industrialization but also fills a gap in our manufacturing of precision grinders.

Before the Great Cultural Revolution, a small number of capitalist roaders in our party and reactionary technical "authorities" had madly suppressed and prevented workers from taking part in designing. Around 1958, there was a group of workers who were promoted to technicians, but, under various pretexts, reactionary "authorities" at the plant gradually transferred them out of the Department of Design. Despite all this, the technicians who came from the ranks of the workers overcame all obstacles and demonstrated their ingenuity and creativity. According to statistics, since 1958, of all the new products designed at the plant, those successfully trial-produced by technicians from the ranks of workers, and by young technicians in collaboration with workers, amounted to 60 per cent in 1958, 70 per cent in 1959, and 80 per cent in 1960. Since 1960, particularly since the start of the Great Proletarian Cultural

Revolution, almost all of the new products were designed and successfully trial-produced by their joint efforts. Not a few of these products meet advanced international standards, e.g., the universal cylindrical grinding machine for mirror surface grinding, the high center cylindrical grinding machine, and other major products.

Some young technicians with college degrees have gradually shaken off the influence of revisionist educational policy, cast off their privileged status, and collaborated with workers. After a period of practice, they also made some more meaningful contributions in designing and trial-production. For instance, a 1964 college graduate always kept a foreign book on the thread grinding machine when he first began work at the plant. (The fact that we mention his foreign book does not mean that we should not read them.) Proceeding from theory to theory, he did not accomplish anything at work. During the Great Cultural Revolution, he raised his class consciousness and understanding of the struggle between the proletarian revolutionary line and the bourgeois reactionary line, and he decided to follow the road of integrating with workers. Early this year, together with two technicians who came from the ranks of workers and a veteran worker, he successfully trial-produced an important electric device for grinders.

Why do technicians promoted from the ranks of workers develop faster and contribute more?

The most important reason is that they have deep proletarian feelings toward Chairman Mao and the Communist Party. They do not work for fame and wealth, they are not afraid of dangers and hardships, and they will not stop working until they reach their goal. They firmly remember Chairman Mao's teachings and always think about how to compete favorably, in speed and quality, with the imperialists, revisionists, and reactionaries. Furthermore, they constantly try to find ways to economize resources for the state and to make the production process easy and efficient for workers. Some of the young intellectuals, however, affected by the poisonous influence of the revisionist educational policy, have long ago separated themselves from productive labor, alienated themselves from the workers, and longed for bourgeois fame and wealth; and they accomplished nothing in the end. There was one technician who dreamed of achieving fame as an expert in one brilliant move; he worked on some sixty research projects over the last ten years, which he gave up one after the other, thus inflicting a great financial loss on the state. Aiming at building up a reputation for himself, a 1956 college graduate did experiments on grinding heads all alone, and he ruined altogether some thirty grinding heads. At long last, he asked veteran workers to help him. With their assistance, he finally succeeded in his experiments. In retrospect, he said: "Trying to make a grinding head behind closed doors only makes one suffer from complete failure. By working together with the workers, one tastes the sweetness of success. In the final analysis, one has to grind his own head first before he knows how to make a good grinding head."

There is a much sharper contrast between technicians promoted from the ranks of workers and the traditional fame and wealth-hungry bourgeois intellectuals. There was a bourgeois "expert" who spent eight years and a large amount of state capital in designing a grinder and failed completely. In the process, he collected quite a bit of so-called "data," which he used as capital to create fame and wealth for himself. About this the workers said, "How can such people have any feeling for our new society?"

Chairman Mao says: "The wisest and the ablest are those fighters who have practical experience." This is because, in their long period of practical work, they have accumulated a great deal of experience and because, after a few years of study in the after-work schools or in spare-time specialized technical institutes, they have closely integrated theory and practical work. Thus they have achieved a "leap forward" in knowledge, enabling them to successfully conduct scientific research and make independent designs. This is an extremely important reason why they become creative so much faster.

When they study, they do so to solve particular problems. Therefore, they penetrate, understand, and know how to apply the things they learn. Using his rich experience in practical work, one technician solved very complex technical problems in developing a product. While working on his product and studying the theory of metal-cutting, which he rapidly absorbed, he developed his own methods and ideas in metal-cutting processing.

Before they integrate with workers, it is very difficult for technicians who graduated from colleges and universities to produce anything, because of their inadequate practical experience and the irrelevancy of their book knowledge to productive work. For example, once several technicians of this type designed an internal thread-grinding machine. Because of their inexperience, it was impossible for the workers to assemble the machine from the blueprint until experienced workers revamped some of the parts.

The combination of the revolutionary spirit, which calls for the courage to imagine, to create, and to break through, with a strict scientific approach is an extremely important prerequisite for engineering and technical personnel in scaling scientific and technological heights. Yet to do this is something closely related to one's world outlook and practical experience. Many technicians who come from the ranks of workers have dared to break away from superstitions and foolish traditions, and therefore have become the least conservative, because of their freedom from the mental yoke of personal fame and wealth and because of their rich experience in practical work. A good example of this is the recently trial-produced precision grinder that meets advanced international standards. Because technicians who had come from the ranks of workers had the courage to break out from the obsolescent structure of operations, they reduced the time for making the prototype from eighteen months to six. They also raised the surface finish by four grades, and reduced the number of parts and the total weight by one-third. The product cost was only 15.5 per cent of a foreign-made precision grinder. But some school-trained technicians find it hard to discard superstitions and foolish traditions, and to develop new techniques, because they ignore ideological reform, are always concerned about their personal gains and losses, such as the loss of face and the image of a specialist, and because they have more mental restrictions and reservations than other people. Even they themselves say, "The more books one reads, the tighter his yoke. The result is that he loses his initiative and drive."

Workers at the Shanghai Machine Tool Plant prefer students from the secondary technical schools, if they have to choose between graduates from colleges and graduates of secondary technical schools. Although the latter have less book knowledge, they also have less self-important manners; they have more practical experience and less mental reservations and restrictions created by old or foreign ideas. For these reasons there are quite a number of graduates of secondary technical schools who have accomplished more than graduates of universities. A case in point is the design of two extremely efficient automatic production lines by two 1956 graduates of secondary technical schools.

## THE DIRECTION OF THE EDUCATIONAL REVOLUTION AS SEEN FROM THIS PLANT

On the basis of an analysis of their current conditions and the route that the various types of engineering and technical personnel at the Shanghai Machine Tool Plant have followed, we also can clarify the problem of direction in the revolution in education.

From their experience, veteran workers and many young technicians more thoroughly realize that Chairman Mao's instruction, "the control of our schools by bourgeois intellectuals must not be allowed to continue any longer," is unprecedentedly brilliant and correct. They all believe that it is urgent and significant to carry out the proletarian revolution in education according to Chairman Mao's educational ideas. His series of instructions on revolution in education point out our forward direction. Now, our problem is to act firmly and thoroughly, as Chairman Mao instructs.

In accordance with Chairman Mao's ideas on education and the special conditions at the plant, workers and technicians have presented the following views and suggestions regarding the revolution in education.

1. Schools must educate, as Chairman Mao instructs, "workers with socialist consciousness and culture." This is unlike the schools under the control of revisionist educational policies, which trained "intellectual aristocrats" who were alienated from proletarian politics, the broad masses of workers and peasants, and production work. This is a fundamental question affecting whether revisionism is to be wiped out or not. Comrades at the Shanghai Machine Tool Plant believe that, in the past, it was a mistake to assign new graduates of colleges and universities as cadres in factories and in the countryside. The integration of young students with workers and peasants and the participation of the former in productive labor are an important means of changing their world outlook and teaching them practical, technical knowledge. Therefore, they recommend that new graduates of colleges and universities should, first of all, be assigned as ordinary laborers in factories and in the countryside, to take part in productive labor. They should earn their "qualification certificates" from workers and peasants, and then, depending upon actual demands, some of them may be assigned as technicians; but they must still devote a certain amount of time to physical labor. The rest will continue as ordinary workers and peasants.

2. School education must be combined with productive labor. Chairman Mao instructs that "our main method is to learn how to fight from fighting." Judging from the conditions of some of the technicians at the Shanghai Machine Tool Plant, one of the serious weaknesses of the old educational system was the separation of theory from practice and the overemphasis on ab-

stract traditional doctrines and methods, which made those who read more all the more stupid. Only by doing practical work can one master theory quickly and thoroughly, and apply it creatively. For this reason, workers and technicians at this point recommend that schools appoint experienced workers as teachers; that workers be allowed to lecture; and that some of the subjects be taught by workers right in the workshops. There was a young technician who was assigned to work in a research office right after his graduation from the university. All day long he devoured books and deeply immersed himself in theory and in studying foreign languages. Because he was completely isolated from production work, he felt frustrated all the time. In the early stage of the Great Cultural Revolution, he went to learn from workers at the machine tool plant who had had a lot of experience; he worked on the bench and things began to change for him. Recently, working together with ordinary workers, he made a meaningful contribution in the grinding of a mirror surface. He is now thoroughly convinced that he must have workers as his teachers.

3. With regard to the source of engineering and technical personnel, they believe, that, in addition to continuing to promote workers to become technicians, units should also select graduates of junior and senior high schools who have sound political ideology and two to three, or four to five, years of experience in productive labor, and send them to study in junior colleges and universities. There is now every possibility to do so. Take the Shanghai Machine Tool Plant as an example. Most of its workers have an education above junior high school. The advantages of selecting these youths to study in colleges and universities are: (a) they have a better political background; (b) they have a proven ability to do practical work, and experience in productive labor; (c) after a few years of work, a graduate of junior or senior high school is about twenty years old. After another few years of study he will be graduated at age twenty-three or twenty-four, and will be able to work independently. As of now, a graduate of a university

generally will be able to work independently only after two to three years of internship. Therefore, it is entirely consistent with the principle of getting more, quicker, better, and more economical results to send youths with practical experience to study in universities.

4. As regards the retraining and raising of the standard of the existing technical force at the plant, they point out the fact that a large number of technicians graduated from various schools have long been subjected to the evil influence of revisionist educational policy and revisionist policy in managing economic enterprises. In addition, there is a group of technicians who were trained before the liberation of China. Some of them naturally are patriotic, and are working very hard; they are not antiparty or antisocialist, and are not loyal to any foreign country, but they do have many problems regarding their world outlook and work style. In accordance with the policy outlined in the "Decision of the Central Committee of the Communist Party of China on the Great Proletarian Cultural Revolution," the plant should hold high the great banner of revolutionary criticism, as advocated by Mao Tse-tung's thought, and organize them to participate in the revolutionary criticism meetings. These technicians will learn, in their mass meetings, how to thoroughly denounce such fallacies of China's Khrushchev as "experts should manage the factories" and "putting techniques in command," as well as the attitudes of "go slow" and "unconditionally accept anything foreign as better." They will also learn how to thoroughly repudiate the bourgeois idea of seeking fame and wealth. Meanwhile, the plant should organize their technicians into groups and send them, from time to time, to work as ordinary workers; or just arrange for them to have more time to work in the workshops as part of their regular everyday job, so as to assist them to integrate with workers and to combine theory and practical work.

# 12: A New Type of School That Combines Theory with Practice

*This investigation report on the Wukow Part-Time Tea-Growing and Part-Time Study Middle School in Wuyuan County, Kiangsi Province, appeared in* Hung Ch'i (Red Flag), *no. 4, 1968. It was prepared by the communications section of the Wuyuan Revolutionary Committee, a* New Shang-yao Daily *reporter, and the* Kiangsi Daily *Shang-yao reporter unit.*

## RED FLAG *EDITOR'S NOTE*

This article was originally printed in the *Kiangsi Daily* [September 11, 1968]. With some minor changes, it is reprinted here for our readers' reference. This school has only four full-time teachers (with one of them in charge). Other teachers are part-time; they are workers, tea-growers, and technicians who were promoted from among the workers. This system works out very well. Can this experience be adopted in all city schools? Although how to select students from poor and lower-middle peasants was not discussed in the article, rather good experiences have been recorded in other sources. Judging from this experience, it is possible to put Chairman Mao's proletarian revolutionary educational ideology into practice faster in the villages than in other areas; this is because it is easier for the schools in the villages to establish the supremacy of poor and lower-middle peasants. This experience further proves how necessary it is to send workers' Mao Tse-tung's thought propaganda teams, including People's Liberation Army personnel, to all schools in the cities. Those of us who still have reservations about this policy had better study the conditions in the villages.

* * *

The purpose of the following article is to introduce the experience in educational reform at the Wukow Part-Time Tea-Growing and Part-Time Study Middle School in Wuyuan County. This school was established in 1965. At the beginning, it was not clear what line of policy and what direction the school should follow. To discuss this problem, the tea plantation and school authorities called several meetings. At these meetings, veteran tea workers and tea-growers, who were invited to attend, all spoke. They pointed out the danger created by the old tea plantation's vocational and technical schools during the old days as a result of their deviation from proletarian politics, their divorce from the workers and peasants, their separation from physical labor. They also condemned the criminal actions of the bourgeois educational policy. The poor and lower-middle peasants strongly demanded that "our proletarian school must not be run like the old schools under the control of capitalists in the past. They turned our children into useless youths who could not carry anything on their shoulders and who could not carry anything in their hands." We must follow Chairman Mao's instructions to train "working people who have socialist consciousness and culture." After this meeting, plantation and school authorities, on their own initiative, invited tea plantation workers and poor and lower-middle peasants to play a role in leading and managing the school. They have vigorously strengthened the workers' political-ideological leadership in the school by inviting the latter to attend, to criticize, and to voice their opinions and suggestions whenever there is a discussion of school policies. In addition, representatives of plantation workers and local poor and lower-middle peasants have become members of the school revolutionary committee. Thus, with the active participation of these workers and peasants, the plantation and school authorities have been gradually carrying out educational reform in accordance with Chairman Mao's proletarian policy.

## HOW DOES THIS NEW TYPE
## OF SCHOOL TEACH?

Under the leadership and management of the workers and the poor and lower-middle peasants, the Wukow Part-Time Tea-Growing and Part-Time Study Middle School in Wuyuan County has opened a new avenue of reform in teaching.

The overriding principle of educational reform at this school is to establish the dominance of proletarian politics, to use Mao Tse-tung's thought to dictate everything, to simplify and to improve the curriculum, and to closely integrate learning with productive labor so as to put knowledge to practical use.

The salient features of the educational reform in this school are: the students leave their classrooms and accept workers and peasants as their teachers; they use workshops and farms as their classrooms, thus integrating learning with production; they not only learn to produce tea on the tea plantation but also learn general farming in the fields. Because of the very close integration of learning with productive work, the students learn fast, they retain what they have learned, and they know how to apply whatever they have learned.

1. *Most enthusiastically study Chairman Mao's teachings.* The school authorities issued every teacher and student a copy of the *Selected Readings From Mao Tse-tung's Writings.* They dropped the regular Chinese language courses; in language courses, as in the courses in political education, Chairman Mao's writings, particularly the latest series of instructions and the directives on educational reform, became the special textbooks.

Different kinds of Mao Tse-tung's thought study classes have been organized, including those sponsored by the school, by a class, by a production platoon or squad, and by a dormitory. All squads, platoons, or classes hold their meetings once a week to discuss their study and application of Chairman Mao's thought. In this way, they have truly given top priority to the study of Chairman Mao's writings.

Furthermore, the school has put great stress on class education. For example, it uses as subjects of discussion cases from the local class struggle, which reflect the plots of rich landlords, reactionaries, and subversive rightists, and the many criminal acts of counterrevolutionaries in undermining the school's plan to "resume classes while carrying on the revolution in the school." All this helps to raise the understanding of the class struggle and the conflicts between the two opposing ideologies, and to inspire a proletarian spirit, in order to motivate better study and better use of Chairman Mao's thought in re-shaping perspectives on the world.

2. *Thoroughly understand the struggle between the two opposing lines in education; simplify cumbersome teaching material and make it serve practical needs.* Traditionally, tea-growing plantation schools conducted their instruction in classrooms. Very rarely did students have anything to do with production. The curriculums then were extremely complicated, trivial, and impractical. At the beginning, at the Wukow Part-Time Tea-Growing and Part-Time Study School, the curriculum in the department of tea-growing alone comprised twelve courses. In addition, there were a number of basic courses in mathematics, physics, and chemistry, which were all required. How could the students handle such an enormous load of twenty-one courses? It turned out that some had knowledge they had learned but could not use; and they had not learned what they needed to use. This was an extreme waste of the energy and time of the students and teachers. But, because of the strong influence of the counterrevolutionary revisionist educational line and the useless ideology of others, some teachers were quite conservative about a reform of the curriculum. As a result, some mathematics teachers continued to teach their courses in the traditional way.

Some foreign language teachers wanted to add more foreign language courses. Some chemistry teachers wanted to show off their "expertise" so badly that every time they had to write chemical formulas, they filled up the whole blackboard before they stopped. Yet all these formulas had nothing to do with tea-growing.

There is no construction without destruction. Aiming at eliminating these obstacles, tea plantation and school authorities organized a large number of Mao Tse-tung's thought study classes in which students and teachers relentlessly criticized the counterrevolutionary, revisionist educational policy of China's Khrushchev. At the criticism meeting, Comrade Chu Chin-kwei, who had worked for a number of years at the old part-time tea-growing and part-time study college, said furiously: "The old education was nothing more than the feudal, capitalist, and revisionist stuff. Most of the students it turned out were full of ideas of seeking fame and wealth, and they knew nothing but useless theories. After three years of tea-growing school, the first grade tea they were supposed to produce actually turned out to be third grade. Today, if we still take the old road of going to school in order to become bureaucrats and to achieve fame and make big money, assuming that those with higher grades are better students, then we are really being fooled by China's Khrushchev. If we let landlords and bourgeoisie lead us by our noses, we will forget our proletarian character. We must absolutely never do such a thing." Such a strong indictment by this veteran worker of the old system is a real education for everybody.

After raising revolutionary understanding, the school leadership issued timely calls to students and teachers to face real life, to leave the classrooms, to hold classes in the workshops and tea plantation, and against this background, to evaluate the teaching materials, to reassess the curriculum, and to decide what to discard and what to retain in an effort to reform education.

This thorough, empirical approach has produced some desirable results. Judging by their practical needs, and in compliance with the principle that education must serve tea-growing and agriculture, students and teachers put together all the complicated but trivial teaching materials, which seemed to be unrelated, simplified them, and made some of them into concise manuals. Since the completion of this project, the current special courses for tea-growing have been reduced to two from the previous twelve, and the courses in mathematics, physics, and chemistry have also been greatly simplified. Both the students and teachers are very happy about this reform.

3. *Welcome workers and peasants as teachers, as "barefoot teachers giving lectures"; intellectuals and young students integrate with workers and peasants; establish a three-way combination of workers, peasants, and students for teaching and learning.* This school only has four full-time teachers (including one who is in charge). All other teachers are part-time—plantation workers, tea-growers, and technicians who were promoted from ordinary workers. Workshops, tea gardens, and farm fields have also been used as classrooms for teaching the planting and processing of tea leaves and the cultivating of other agricultural produce. All these arrangements have become institutionalized. With their great experience in production work, workers and peasants, when they teach, know how to explain things vividly in simple terms. They are most enthusiastically received by the students. Many students commented: "From workers and peasants we have learned many things that we could not have learned in the classrooms in the past." And they say: "Listening to veteran workers explain the lessons to us in the workshops, it is so much easier to understand, to absorb, and to apply the things we learned." Some teachers said: "In the past, when we lectured about diesel engines, even after seven or eight hours of instruction, it was still difficult to get the main ideas across. When we touched on the second part of the lectures, the students had already forgotten about the first part. Now it takes veteran workers at the plantation less than an hour to thoroughly explain everything. And

they take the machines apart and put them back together without any trouble whatsoever.

4. *Participate in production work and learn through
physical labor.* This school also underwent quite a struggle in implementing the policy that "education must
serve proletarian politics and must be integrated with
production labor." At the beginning, there were teachers
who did not want to take part in production work because they were afraid of difficulties and physical exer-
tion. Some teachers said: "I came to teach, not to do
physical labor." Some students had the same attitude.
To combat this negative idea, tea plantation and school
authorities started to organize teacher and student
groups to study Chairman Mao's teachings and selections from his quotations on this subject. Chairman Mao
says: "Working people should master intellectual work
and intellectuals should also engage in manual work."
He also says: "By taking part in collective production
labor, the cadres maintain extensive, constant, and close
ties with the working people. This is a major measure
of fundamental importance for a socialist system; it helps
to overcome bureaucracy and to prevent revisionism and
dogmatism." After the study campaign, there was a general improvement in the ideological understanding on
the part of the teachers and students in the school. Now
they follow the example of K'ang-ta in doing productive labor while studying, and in the spirit of hard work
and extreme austerity in which the college was run.
Therefore, teachers and students have developed a revolutionary attitude toward hard work and have firmly
adhered to the idea of integrating education with productive labor.

Usually this means that they insist what they do and
study be closely related to local productive work. For
example, from August every year until April the following year, when there is an off-season in the tea-growing
areas, the primary task of the students and teachers is
to open up new land and bring it into the tea plantation, and to rejuvenate and transplant tea shrubs. Thus,
the school emphasizes a new combination of learning

and working through surveying and laying out of tea gardens, designing preliminary tea-processing workshops, and learning the techniques of cultivating and transplanting tea shrubs. Students learn while working and work while learning. There is less classroom instruction and more actual work in the field.

During the busy season, in addition to daily manual work, classes are conducted in the tea gardens and tea-processing shops, where students and teachers learn from workers and peasants through doing work. This year, the plantation had a good harvest, thus there was plenty of tea-picking and processing. Teachers and students, therefore, volunteered to pick and to process tea leaves. For two months, the students tried hard to learn from plantation workers complete dedication to the state, and love for hard work and simple living. At the same time, they absorbed a great deal of technical knowledge and working experience. They were successful both in learning and work, competently completing the processing of more than one hundred tons of tea leaves on time. As a result, they have vigorously supported the production of the tea plantation and contributed to the nation's socialist construction work.

### NEW TYPE OF SCHOOL GROOMS SUCCESSORS FOR THE PROLETARIAN REVOLUTIONARY TASKS

Under the direction of Chairman Mao's proletarian educational policy, the working class leads the school, and the poor and lower-middle peasants run the school. This gives this new type of school a healthy atmosphere and wholesome work style. The more than one hundred young students at the Wukow Part-Time Tea-Growing and Part-Time Study School are being developed into "workers having socialist consciousness and culture." Not only have the young students been healthily growing in learning, guided by the masses of workers and peasants, but also the teachers at the school have been accepting workers and peasants as their own teachers, traveling on the road of integrating with workers and peasants.

With unbounded loyalty toward Chairman Mao and toward the proletarian headquarters, which is headed by Chairman Mao with Vice Chairman Lin Piao as his deputy, the teachers and students have been closely following Chairman Mao's great strategy, carrying out every one of his latest instructions and opposing the reactionary theory of "many centers, meaning no centers," and many other reactionary bourgeois ideas. They have a very firm stand, and they demonstrate clearly what they are for and what they are against. They follow Chairman Mao's great instruction to "never forget class struggle," thus unwaveringly and courageously fighting against the enemy. They regularly walk many miles a night to go to the plantation headquarters and the different communes nearby to join the poor and the lower-middle peasants in their struggle against class enemies. One day, when they discovered that there was a counter-revolutionary hiding in the mountains, they went to capture him. Armed with Chairman Mao's thought, the entire student body and faculty launched a thorough and lasting revolutionary criticism campaign in order to expose and to denounce China's Khrushchev, his agent Fang Chih-chung, and their followers' counter-revolutionary crimes, to criticize the counterrevolutionary, revisionist educational policy of China's Khrushchev, and to repudiate the bourgeois attitude of despising the workers and peasants. In doing so, they have shown unlimited enmity toward the class enemies and have displayed unlimited love for workers and poor and lower-middle peasants. When they found that a path connecting the school and the bank of a little river was in bad condition, causing quite a bit of inconvenience to the workers and peasants, the students repaired it voluntarily. There was an old, poor woman peasant, a member of the Wukow Production Brigade. While her sons were away from her for a period of time, the students brought water to her, chopped wood and planted vegetables for her. Every time the students saw the workers and peasants pulling their carts up and down a little slope near the school, they never failed to run to them, offering a helping hand like class brothers.

They live a simple life, and they work very hard with a selfless spirit. Three years have elapsed since the founding of the school, and they have been persistent in following the example of K'ang-ta; they compile and print their own teaching materials, and they manage to get along with only a little teaching equipment. Like the old Red Army personnel, they even cut their own hair, do their own laundry, repair their own clothes, and repair their own desks and chairs. In the teacher's quarters, there is only one bed, one desk, and a few stools. They plant vegetables and raise hogs for their own needs. As a result of their vigorous productive labor, this year they are not only completely self-sufficient, without spending one single cent of state funds, but they also have a surplus in their budget.

Thus, this school turns out students who are pure in ideology, good in study, strong in productive labor, and correct in work style.

There was a student named Cheng Wei-shih who enrolled in the school in 1966. After less than three days she wanted to go home because she didn't want to do manual labor. She said: "It is a loss of face to do manual labor in school." The first time she was assigned to pull tea bushes, she got several blisters with a little blood after she did only a tiny bit of work. When she was sent to chop wood, while every worker and peasant who went along collected a full load, she only had seven kilograms. Upon return, she was sore all over; lying in bed, she could not even eat that day. Schoolmates dubbed her "the delicate young lady." There was, however, after a period of education and tempering, a fundamental change in her thinking. In the past, when she had seen the peasants carrying nightsoil, she would cover up her nose even at quite a distance. Now, together with her schoolmates, she regularly carries nightsoil and plants vegetables. In April of this year, while she was on leave visiting her family, her mother said, "Wei-shih, your brother is home on leave from his military unit. This is a rare reunion. So you should also stay a few more days and keep your brother company. You don't need to do any work at home." She promised her mother perfunctorily. But, as soon as her mother was away, she joined the commune members in manual labor. Everybody complimented her, saying: "Since Wei-shih has gone to the part-time tea-growing and part-time study school, she has improved a great deal. Now she can do both mental and manual work—indeed, she is a good student of Chairman Mao."

The masses of workers and peasants can best judge what kind of school trains what kind of students, and which school is good and which is bad. Yu Ching-hung and her cousin came from poor peasant families. After they graduated from primary school, the former passed the entrance examination and was admitted to the part-time tea-growing and part-time study middle school, while the latter went to a regular middle school. When they were small, both had the same ideas about things. But they became two different kinds of students after the training in two different kinds of schools. Yu made progress in political ideology in leaps and bounds. She was elected many times as an activist in the living study and application of Chairman Mao's thought; and she attended the meetings, sponsored by the tea plantation and the county, of representatives of activists in the living study and application of Chairman Mao's thought. She cherishes unlimited affection for Chairman Mao, saying frequently, "Chairman Mao is the savior of us poor and lower-middle peasants. Only when there is Chairman Mao can we poor and lower-middle peasants have anything of our own to speak of. If it were not for his leading us to liberate ourselves from the bourgeois reactionaries, I'd never be able to go to school. Now that we are free, we cannot forget who helped us become free. Therefore, we must be loyal to Chairman Mao and follow him in carrying out his revolution forever and ever." On the other hand, what has happened to her cousin? He changed, all right: he wore more elegant clothes and his skin became whiter. When he first entered the middle school, he occasionally did some manual labor while visiting home. Later, he did not bother to do anything. The villagers who saw the changes in these two students all said: "The tea-growing school is fine. It is a good school for us poor and lower-middle peasants. It costs the state nothing to study there. Yet, it certainly turns out solid students."

The students have not only made big progress politically and ideologically, they have also gained rapidly in specialized knowledge. Now they not only have theoretical knowledge but they also have practical skill. When they entered the tea-growing school, they knew little about tea production. Now they are quite familiar with planting tea shrubs, managing tea gardens, killing plant diseases and insect pests, and picking and processing tea leaves.

Now students of the 1965 class are trained to participate in planning tea gardens, designing tea-processing workshops, and installing machinery. The fact is that they are far better than the graduates of the tea vocational middle schools. The principal of this school was a technician promoted from among the workers at the old tea plantation. He came here to work soon after he was graduated from the Central China Tea Vocational School in 1954. He compares himself with the students in his school today by saying that then, except for some book knowledge, he knew nothing about the cultivation and processing of teas or the designing of a tea-processing workshop, let alone the installing of machinery. Only later, following Chairman Mao's instruction to integrate with workers and peasants, did he very humbly ask the workers and peasants to teach him from scratch. It was then that he gradually learned his trade and related techniques. So he concluded that his real teachers were workers and peasants. He often tells people about his own experience, saying: "Workers and peasants are our parents. And they are always our teachers. If we want to learn some skills to serve the people, we must follow Chairman Mao's advice to accept workers and peasants as our teachers and follow the road of integrating with them."

In commending the students of this school, the local poor and lower-middle peasants said: "They are truly the students of us farmers. Such a younger generation is really solid and reliable. We have no worry about them." People in many places in the county are regularly trying to find out when this school will admit new students. All poor and lower-middle peasants want to send their children to this school.

Chairman Mao teaches us: "The period of schooling should be shortened, education should be revolutionized, and the domination of our schools by bourgeoisie intellectuals should by no means be allowed to continue."

Recently, Chairman Mao again penetratingly pointed out for us: "To accomplish the proletarian revolution in education, it is essential to have working class leadership; the masses of workers must take part in this revolution and, in cooperation with Liberation Army fighters, form a revolutionary three-in-one combination with the activists among the students, teachers, and workers in schools and colleges who are determined to carry the proletarian revolution in education through to the end. The worker propaganda teams should stay permanently in the schools and colleges, take part in all the struggle–criticism–transformation tasks there, and always lead these institutions. In the countryside, schools and colleges should be managed by the poor and lower-middle peasants—the most reliable allies of the working class."

The experience of the Wukow Part-Time Tea-Growing and Part-Time Study Middle School in Wuyuan County has proved how great and how brilliant Chairman Mao's instructions have been. It also has shown that such new schools, which integrate theory with practical work, and as created and promoted by Chairman Mao, can be instituted throughout the country. The high tide of the educational revolution for the entire province and for the whole country is here.

# 13: Taking All Society As Their Factory: Peking University's Achievements in Educational Revolution in the Liberal Arts

*From* Peking Review, *no. 5 (February 2, 1973).*

Having gone through the Great Proletarian Cultural Revolution, Peking University is developing into a new-type socialist university. It has seventeen departments embracing over sixty specialties and a teaching staff of more than two thousand. Since August 1970, it has enrolled some four thousand students from among young workers, peasants, and soldiers with practical experience all over the country. This is something unheard of in the old-type universities.

The liberal arts in Peking University, which is located in the northwestern suburbs of the capital, include Chinese, history, philosophy, political economy, international politics, law, and library science departments. Chairman Mao has pointed out: "The liberal arts should take all society as their factory." Like the science and engineering colleges which have their own factories or establish contacts with local plants to enable teachers and students to link study with actual production, the liberal arts teachers and students, apart from class work, devote some time every year to taking part in class struggle and productive labor in factories, people's communes, PLA units, and shops and making social investigations, stressing theoretical study based on practice. Good results have thus been obtained in educational revolution.

Prior to the Great Cultural Revolution, Chairman Mao time and again called on the liberal arts teachers and students to go among the workers and peasants and learn how to make revolution by taking part in class struggle. He clearly pointed out: "Education must serve proletarian politics and be combined with productive labor." However, Liu Shao-ch'i and his agents in the field of education pushed a revisionist line in a futile bid to lead teachers and students astray, making them divorce themselves from proletarian politics, the worker and peasant masses, and productive labor.

## PROFOUND CHANGES

Repudiation of this counterrevolutionary revisionist line in education during the Cultural Revolution has enabled the students and teachers in the college of liberal arts to embark on the road of taking all society as their factory, thereby drastically changing the teaching system.

Since two years ago, they have incorporated their study in and out of the university. While attending classes, students concentrate their time and energy in systematically studying the basic knowledge of the various subjects they major in. Together with their teachers, they are out in society four months a year, applying what they have learned to practice. In this way, the old bookish way of study has been done away with, and the students' ability to use Marxist theory to analyze and solve problems has been raised.

In 1971 the students in the Chinese department specializing in literature and their teachers went to a production brigade in Miyun *hsien* on Peking's outskirts to do some investigation work. The heroic deeds of Liu Mao-ching, the brigade's late Party branch secretary who had led the peasants in building a socialist new countryside, inspired them to do creative writing. While tutoring students in such writing, the teachers lectured on the relevant parts of such courses as the Marxist theory of literature and art, writing methods, analysis of classical and modern literary works, and grammar and rhetoric and organized the students to conscientiously study Chairman Mao's *Talks at the Yenan Forum on Literature and Art* and other works. The result was the students wrote a collection of revolutionary stories.

In cooperation with the Peking Historical Relics Administration, teachers and students in archaeology under the history department unearthed a Western Chou dynasty (c. 1066–771 B.C.) village and discovered three-thousand-year-old houses, kitchen ranges, pottery, and other things. This initial training in field excavation helped extend their knowledge of what had been learned in the classroom.

The Ming Tombs in Changping *hsien* on Peking's northwestern outskirts, where thirteen Ming emperors are buried, became lecture rooms on the history of the Ming dynasty (1368–1644 A.D.) and the Ch'ing dynasty 1644–1911 A.D.). Teachers and students read historical data, visited the luxurious underground mausoleum of a Ming emperor and his wife, and investigated the family histories of the peasants living in the locality for generations. What they found spoke volumes for the harsh exploitation and oppression of the peasants by the feudal rulers and the former's resistance and struggle. This was very conducive to grasping Marxist historical materialism and using the theory of class struggle to study historical problems and criticize the idealist concept of history.

## FROM ABSTRACT CONCEPTS TO WEAPONS OF STRUGGLE

Before the Great Cultural Revolution began, the philosophy department did not regard philosophy as a subject in which the students study theory to carry out class struggle and serve proletarian politics. Instead, it confined philosophy to textbooks and the classroom and asked the students to learn only some philosophical concepts from books. The situation has now fundamentally changed.

In conjunction with the study of the basic theories of historical materialism, one hundred fifty teachers and students of the philosophy department in the third year not long ago spent one and a half months carrying out social investigations in several factories, shops and schools and among the inhabitants in the capital's western district. They put the stress on investigating the management system of industrial enterprises, class struggle in commercial departments, education among children and youngsters, and other questions, in the course of which the students raised many practical and theoretical questions, such as the law of class struggle in the period of socialism, the features and law of struggle between the proletariat and the bourgeoisie in influencing and winning over the younger generation. With the teachers' guidance, they read and studied hard and strove to use the Marxist stand, viewpoint, and method to answer these questions. In addition to over sixty fact-finding reports and study notes by individuals, they joined efforts to write more than thirty investigation reports.

To gain a deeper understanding of the Marxist theory of knowledge, a group of teachers and students from the same department visited the Yungting Machinery Plant, where experienced workers had through collective efforts created a new-type drill bit. Their aim was to analyze, in the light of this technical innovation, such reactionary fallacies as idealist apriorism spread by Liu Shao-ch'i and other political swindlers and to find out typical examples of workers' applying the materialist theory of reflection in practice. On the basis of investigations, the students carried out mass revolutionary criticism together with the workers. Meanwhile, they earnestly restudied *Theses on Feuerbach, Ludwig Feuerbach and the End of Classical German Philosophy*, some chapters of *Anti-Dühring* and *Materialism and Empirico-Criticism* and other works by Marx, Engels, Lenin, and Stalin and Chairman Mao's works like *On Practice* and *Where Do Man's Correct Ideas Come From?*

Teachers gave on-the-spot lectures on the basic viewpoints of the Marxist theory of knowledge. Before they came to the plant, some students had had some muddled ideas about the origin of man's knowledge and talent. During discussions and criticism meetings, the workers repudiated idealist apriorism which had been advertised by Liu Shao-ch'i and other political swindlers, together with fatalism spread by the exploiting classes in the old society, pinpointing the fact that idealist apriorism was nothing but mental shackles used by the reactionary ruling classes for enslaving the people. Recounting her own experience of knowing nothing about technique at first and becoming a master of her line, a woman lathe operator explained that talent came only from practice. All this was a profound education for the students.

## LIVELY PEDAGOGIC ACTIVITIES

When studying the road of development for socialist agriculture, the students in the political-economy department read Engels' *The Peasant Question in France and Germany,* Lenin's *On Cooperation,* and Chairman Mao's works on agricultural cooperation. Afterward the teachers took them to several people's communes with different characteristics to carry out social surveys. While in Hsipu Production Brigade (see *Peking Review,* 1972, No. 51) of the Chienming People's Commune in Hopei Province's Tsunhua *hsien,* a brigade commended by Chairman Mao during the movement for agricultural cooperation, they learned about the entire course of agricultural collectivization from old poor peasants and cadres. When the cooperative, which later developed into the present brigade, had been set up it was very poor and owned only three-fourths of a donkey, the sole draught animal shared by a number of peasant households of which one-fourth did not join the co-op. Today farming in this brigade is being mechanized. After reading and collecting a large amount of data, coupled with serious study of Marxist works in the course of investigation, the teachers and students gained a deeper understanding of the Marxist–Leninist theory of cooperation.

Some teachers and students in the international politics department had their lessons on Lenin's *Imperialism, the Highest Stage of Capitalism* in the Mentoukou Coal-Mine, the iron-smelting mill of the Shoutu Iron and Steel Company, and the Shihchingshan Power Plant on Peking's western outskirts. All had been victims of imperialist plunder. While extensively investigating the history of savage imperialist plunder, the teachers and students held forums with veteran workers who accused the imperialists of barbarous exploitation and raised many questions on the current international class struggle. This was an impetus to the teachers and students in their theoretical study and research work. With the help of the teachers, the students extensively read relevant material and at the same time studied Lenin's work. As a result, they arrived at a deep understanding of Lenin's thesis that export of capital is a major characteristic of imperialism. These lively pedagogic activities enabled the students to write four fact-finding reports, including "Plunder of the Mentoukou Coal Mine by the Imperialist Powers," "An Investigation on Imperialist Capital Export in the Shihchingshan Tube-Casting Mill," and "Imperialist Control and Plunder of the Shihchingshan Power Plant."

Taking all society as their factory has brought marked improvement in the quality of teaching to the liberal arts. Speaking of his own experience, a young philosophy teacher said: "I studied philosophy for five years in the old Peking University. When I wrote year-end and graduate theses, I often copied abstract concepts and philosophical jargon. Now with only a little over a year's study, students have begun to use Marxist theory to criticize the bourgeoisie and write articles with clear-cut. views and rich contents. This is a striking contrast between the two lines in education and the results produced."

C. T. Hu, Professor of Comparative Education at Teachers College, Columbia University, received the B.A. degree from Fu-tan University in Chungking, China, and his Ph.D. in history from the University of Washington in 1954. He has taught at Princeton, the University of Delhi, and Harvard. His publications include *China, Its People, Its Society, Its Culture; Aspects of Chinese Education;* and articles in *The China Quarterly, Saturday Review, Yearbook of Education* and many other journals both in the United States and overseas.